ASK THE VET

QUESTIONS & ANSWERS

FOR CAT OWNERS

Gary D. Norsworthy
DVM, Dipl ABVP

ৡ

Sharon K. Fooshee
MS, DVM, Dipl ABVP, Dipl ACVIM

ৡ

With contributions by

R. Charles Povey
BVSc, PhD, FRCVS

ৡ

Illustrations by Rebecca Brebner

A Lifelearn Publication

Lifelearn Inc., Guelph, Ontario, Canada

Project Editor: Anne Behnan
Cover Design: Leah Aurini

ISBN 1-896985-00-9

Disclosure and Caution: Every care has been taken to provide accurate information. However knowledge is not absolute. Medical opinions differ. Drugs are subject to change in dosage, format, etc. The reader is urged to use the information in this book as an adjunct to, and not a substitute for, professional veterinary advice, based on a full and proper examination and knowledge of the patient. To purchase additional copies of this book call 1•800•375•7994 or Fax us at 1•519•767•1101.

PREFACE

Ask the Vet: Questions and Answers for Cat Owners

This book is based on a series of client information sheets that we (G.D.N., S.K.F.) prepared for use in our clinics, and subsequently was developed on disc by Lifelearn as a basis for veterinarians to adapt to their clinic use.

The topics covered are those that are the most frequently encountered health issues in cats. The majority of cats lead very healthy lives, but when they are sick and a visit to a veterinarian is necessary, very little of the doctor's explanation of the illness may be fully understood or remembered. This book will greatly help.

Prevention is better than cure. Many topics covered, such as 'Recommendations for owners of kittens,' 'Dental disease,' 'Special needs of older cats' etc., will provide information as to how and when you can work with your veterinarian to maintain wellness of your pet.

'Emergencies and First Aid' will provide guidance in recognizing true emergencies and dealing with those situations until veterinary help can be obtained.

Gary D. Norsworthy
DVM, Dipl ABVP

Sharon K. Fooshee
MS, DVM, Dipl ABVP, Dipl ACVIM

R. Charles Povey
BVSc, PhD, FRCVS

Cat Skeleton

Coccygeal vertebrae

Metatarsal bones

Fibula

Tibia

Lumbar vertebrae

Femur

Pelvis

Patella

Tarsal bones

Thoracic vertebrae

Rib

Metacarpal bones

Scapula

Cervical vertebrae

Humerus

Ulna

Radius

Sternum

Carpal bones

Mandible

Phalanges

Skull

Table of Contents

I am planning to travel and would like to take my cat with me. What are some of the factors I need to consider before taking my cat on an airplane?

Having your cat along may add enjoyment to your trip. It is important to keep your pet's health and safety in mind when travelling, so be sure to check with the airline well in advance of your trip. Familiarize yourself with the airline's pet requirements so that you can avoid any last minute problems. Here are some basic tips for airline travel with your cat:

- Take direct flights and try to avoid connections and layovers. This eliminates missed baggage connections and the chance that your cat will be left in extreme weather.

- Many airlines will allow one pet in coach and one in first class, with some provisions. Some airlines limit the number of pets travelling within the cabin area so be sure to notify the airline that your cat will be travelling with you. Your cat must be in a standard cage that will fit under the seat and must not disturb your fellow travellers.

- Seek the advice of your veterinarian before travelling. Update all vaccinations. Take all necessary health papers with you. Determine whether a health certificate for the cat will be required at your point of destination. You might also inquire about possible requirements to quarantine your cat should you be travelling to a foreign country.

- Use airlines that hand carry your cat (inside the cage) to and from the aircraft. Otherwise, the cage could simply be placed on a conveyor belt.

- Do not feed your cat for six hours before the flight; allow water until flight time. Water should be available in the cage. Give the cat fresh water as soon as it arrives at the destination.

- Avoid the busiest travel times so airline personnel will have extra time to handle your cat.

- Do not tranquilize your cat without first discussing it with your veterinarian.

- Make sure the cage has specific feeding and identification labels permanently attached.

- Baggage liability limitations apply to your cat. Check your ticket for liability limits or, better yet, speak directly with the airline. If you are sending an economically valuable pet, you may want to purchase additional liability insurance.

- Be aware that airline travel may pose a risk for cats with a pre-existing medical problem. For example, you should give serious thought to travelling by plane with a cat who has kidney disease or heart disease. Also, one study has shown that short-faced breeds of cats (Persians, Exotic Shorthairs) do not travel well in certain situations. Discuss these issues with your veterinarian prior to travel.

What do I need to consider when buying a travel carrier or cage?

Your cat's travel cage will be its "home" for much of your trip. It's important to choose the right cage. Here are some helpful guidelines:

- The cage should be large enough for your cat to stand up and turn around freely.
- The walls of the carrier should be strong and waterproof. This will prevent crushing and waste (urine) leakage.
- There must be adequate ventilation on at least three sides of the cage.
- The cage must have sturdy handles for baggage personnel to use.
- The cage should have a water tray which is accessible from the outside so that water can be added if needed.
- Cover the bottom of the cage with an absorptive covering or underpad. Check with a pharmacy for the flat absorbent underpads designed for bedridden people with bladder control problems.

Pet stores, breeders, and kennels usually sell cages that meet these requirements. Some airlines also sell cages that they prefer to use. Check with the airline to see if they have other requirements.

Try to familiarize your cat with the travel cage before you leave for your trip. Let your cat play inside with the door both open and closed. This will help eliminate some of your cat's stress during the trip.

Is there any other advice which might be useful as I prepare for my trip?

By applying a few common sense rules, you can keep your travelling cat safe and sound.

- Arrange ahead of time to stay in a hotel that allows pets. Many bookstores carry travel guidebooks with this type of information.
- Make sure that your cat wears a collar with an identification tag securely fastened. It should have your name, address, and telephone number.
- Always travel with a leash-harness for your cat. Familiarize your cat with the leash before the trip. Attach your cat's harness while it is still inside the cage. Outside the cage, a frightened cat can easily run away before you have a chance to fasten the leash.
- If you leave your cat unattended in lodging rooms, make sure that there is no opportunity for escape. Leave the cat in the cage or in the bathroom. Be sure to inform housekeeping personnel of your cat and ask that they wait until you return before entering the room. Use "Do Not Disturb" signs.
- Should your pet get lost, contact the local animal control officer.

Remember, advance planning is vital to make the trip an enjoyable experience for both you and your cat.

What are allergies, and how do they affect cats?

One of the most common conditions affecting cats is allergy. In the allergic state, the cat's immune system "overreacts" to foreign substances (allergens or antigens) to which it is exposed. Those overreactions are manifested in three ways. The most common is itching of the skin, either localized (one area) or generalized (all over the cat). Another manifestation involves the respiratory system and may result in coughing, sneezing, and/or wheezing. Sometimes, there may be an associated nasal or ocular (eye) discharge. The third manifestation involves the digestive system, resulting in vomiting or diarrhea.

Are there several types of allergies?

There are four known types of allergies in the cat: contact, flea, food, and inhalant. Each of these has some common expressions in cats, and each has some unique features.

Contact Allergy

Contact allergies are the least common of the four types of allergies. They result in a local reaction on the skin. Examples of contact allergy include reactions to flea collars or to types of bedding, such as wool. If the cat is allergic to those, there will be skin irritation and itching at the points of contact. Removal of the contact irritant solves the problem. However, identifying the allergen can require some detective work.

Flea Allergy

Flea allergy is common in cats. A normal cat experiences only minor irritation in response to flea bites, often without any itching. The flea allergic cat, on the other hand, has a severe, itch-producing reaction when the flea's saliva is deposited in the skin. Just one bite causes such intense itching that the cat may severely scratch or chew itself, leading to the removal of large amounts of hair. There will often be open sores or scabs on the skin, allowing a secondary bacterial infection to begin. The area most commonly involved is over the rump (just in front of the tail). In addition, the cat may have numerous, small scabs around the head and neck. These scabs are called miliary lesions, a term which was coined because the scabs look like millet seeds.

The most important treatment for flea allergy is to get the cat away from all fleas. Therefore, strict flea control is the backbone of successful treatment. Unfortunately, this is not always possible in warm and humid climates, where a new population of fleas can hatch out every 14 - 21 days. When strict flea control is not possible, injections of corticosteroids (or "cortisone" or "steroids") can be used to block the allergic reaction and give relief. This is often a necessary part of dealing with flea allergies. Fortunately, cats are more resistant to the side-effects of steroids than other species. If a secondary bacterial infection occurs, appropriate antibiotics must be used.

Inhalant Allergy

The most common type of allergy is the inhalant type, or atopy. Cats may be allergic to all of the same inhaled allergens that affect us. These include tree pollens (cedar, ash, oak, etc.), grass pollens (especially Bermuda), weed pollens (ragweed, etc.), molds, mildew, and the house dust mite. Many of these allergies occur seasonally, such as ragweed, cedar, and grass pollens. However, others are with us all the time, such as molds, mildew, and house dust mites. When humans inhale these allergens, we express the allergy as a respiratory problem; it is sometimes called "hay fever." The cat's reaction, however, usually produces severe, generalized itching. In fact, the most common cause of itching in the cat is inhalant allergy.

Most cats that have inhalant allergy react to several allergens. If the number is small and they are the seasonal type, itching may last for just a few weeks at a time during one or two periods of the year. If the number of allergens is large or they are present year-round, the cat may itch constantly.

Treatment depends largely on the length of the cat's allergy season. It involves two approaches. Steroids will dramatically block the allergic reaction in most cases. These may be given orally or by injection, depending on the circumstances. As stated previously, the side-effects of steroids are much less common in cats than in people. If steroids are appropriate for your cat, you will be instructed in their proper use by your veterinarian.

Some cats are helped considerably by a hypoallergenic shampoo. It has been demonstrated that some allergens may be absorbed through the skin. Frequent bathing is thought to reduce the amount of antigen exposure through this route. In addition to removing surface antigen, bathing alone will provide some temporary relief from itching and may allow the use of a lower dose of steroids. Antihistamines are usually of little value in the cat but can be tried.

The second major form of allergy treatment is desensitization with specific antigen injections (or "allergy shots"). Once the specific sources of allergy are identified, very small amounts of the antigen are injected weekly. This is all in an attempt to re-program the body's immune system. It is hoped that as time passes, the immune system will become less reactive to the problem-causing allergens. If desensitization appears to help the cat, injections will continue for several years. For most cats, a realistic goal is for the itching to be significantly reduced in severity; in some cats, itching may completely resolve. Generally, steroids are not used with this treatment protocol. This therapeutic approach is recommended for the middle-aged or older cat that has year round itching caused by inhalant allergy. This approach is not successful with food allergy.

Although desensitization is the ideal way to treat inhalant allergy, it does have some drawbacks and may not be the best choice in certain circumstances and for these reasons:

1) *Cost*: This is the most expensive form of treatment.

2) *Age of Patient*: Because many cats develop additional allergies as they get older, young cats may need to be retested 1 - 3 years later.

3) *Success Rate*: About 50% of cats will have an excellent response. About 25% get partial to good response. About 25% get little or no response. The same statistics are true for people undergoing desensitization.

4) *Food Allergies:* Although tests for food allergy are available, the reliability of the test is so low that it is not recommended at this time. A food trial remains the best diagnostic test for food allergy.

5) *Time of Response:* The time until apparent response may be 2 - 5 months, or longer.

6) *Interference from steroids:* Cats must not receive oral steroids for 2 weeks, or injectable steroids for 6 weeks, prior to testing; these drugs will interfere with the test results.

Food Allergy

Cats are not likely to be born with food allergies. More commonly, they develop allergies to food products they have eaten for a long time. The allergy most frequently develops in response to the protein component of the food; for example, beef, pork, chicken, or turkey. Food allergy may produce any of the clinical signs previously discussed, including itching, digestive disorders, and respiratory distress. Testing is recommended for food allergy when the clinical signs have been present for several months, when the cat has a poor response to steroids, or when a very young cat itches without other apparent causes of allergy. Testing is done with a special hypoallergenic diet. Because it takes at least 8 weeks for all other food products to get out of the system, the cat must eat the special diet exclusively for 8 - 12 weeks (or more). If positive response occurs, you will be instructed on how to proceed. *If the diet is not fed exclusively, it will not be a meaningful test.* This cannot be overemphasized. If any type of table food, treats or vitamins are given, these must be discontinued during the testing period.

Because cats that are being tested for inhalant allergy generally itch year round, a food allergy dietary test can be performed while the inhalant test and antigen preparation are occurring.

When steroids are given, relief should be apparent within 12 - 24 hours. If not, please call your veterinarian. The cat should feel better and itch less for about one month. If an increase in water consumption or urination occurs, please report this to your veterinarian for future reference. These side-effects are common with steroid administration and will go away in a few days without treatment. Return for further evaluation if the first signs of itching recur.

- If a hypoallergenic diet is prescribed for your cat, and if it will not do so readily, mix it 25:75 with the current diet for several days, then gradually increase the special diet to 100%. If this does not work, contact your veterinarian for an alternative plan. Discontinue any chewable treats or vitamins. Table food is not allowed. Offer only distilled water to drink, if that is possible.

- If your cat has a flea allergy, flea control is very important, and should include treating the cat and its environment. Bear in mind that flea allergies often accompany other types of allergies, especially inhalant allergy.

- If your cat has a bacterial skin infection secondary to allergy, then antibiotics, topical medication or a medicated shampoo may be prescribed.

I am aware that people get asthma. I am surprised that cats do, as well.

They do, although it is not always called asthma. It is also called chronic bronchitis, allergic bronchitis, allergic pneumonitis, and eosinophilic pneumonitis. All cats are susceptible to the development of asthma, although the Siamese breed appears to have an increased frequency of the disease. In one study, asthma was most commonly reported in middle-aged female Siamese cats.

Why are there so many names for one disease?

"Asthma" is a term which refers to a sequence of events leading to narrowing of the air passages (bronchi and bronchioles) going down into the lungs. In some cats, problems also develop all the way down to the lungs (pneumonitis). One particular type of white blood cell, the eosinophil, is frequently involved in this sequence of events. The term "allergic" is used because an increase in eosinophil numbers is often associated with an allergic reaction. Although there are many terms for this disease, each reflects some aspect of our understanding of this process.

Is asthma really a form of allergy?

Not always. There is no doubt that some cats have an allergic reaction to antigens which are inhaled. Antigens are microscopic elements (usually proteins) which evoke some activity from the immune system. For other cats the reaction appears more of a response to a respiratory irritant.

What are the clinical signs of feline asthma?

The most common sign is coughing. Not only do affected cats cough, but asthmatic cats often assume a characteristic crouched position with the neck extended. For some cats with asthma, the respiratory noise created by asthma (called "wheezing") is so loud that it may be heard without the aid of a stethoscope.

After an asthmatic attack has taken place, the lungs are very susceptible to infection. When this happens, the cat's appetite will decline, fever may develop, and the breathing often becomes quite labored.

How is asthma diagnosed?

There are several bits of data that help us to identify asthmatic cats.

1) There are only a few diseases that cause cats to cough. Therefore, coughing is strongly suggestive of asthma, especially if it is accompanied by the characteristic stance.

2) Cats that are allergic to pollens will usually have episodes of coughing at predictable times of the year.

3) An elevation of eosinophils in the blood stream or in the air passages is found in about 50% of cats with asthma.

4) There are some important changes seen in the chest x-rays (radiographs) of many asthmatic cats.

5) Cats with asthma will generally respond dramatically to cortisone (steroids).

6) Middle-aged female Siamese cats appear over-represented in studies involving cats with asthma.

7) Some events may trigger an episode of respiratory distress: spraying perfume, air fresheners, or hairspray; changing the litterbox or switching to a different litter (e.g. – perfumed); cigarette smoke in the air.

In summary, asthma is diagnosed by a combination of one or more of the following:

a) A history of previous episodes of asthma.

b) Coughing accompanied by the characteristic asthmatic stance.

c) Coughing that correlates with pollination of local trees, shrubs, or flowers.

d) Coughing which occurs in response to some event.

e) Increased eosinophil numbers in the blood stream or airways.

f) Characteristic changes in lung radiographs.

g) Response to steroids.

Since most cats with asthma do not exhibit all of these findings, several tests may be necessary. In a complete evaluation, other causes of coughing and increased eosinophil numbers may need to be considered.

How is asthma treated?

The ideal way to manage feline asthma is to remove the antigen or irritant from the cat's environment. However, first, the offending agent must be identified. If the onset of respiratory distress correlates with the blooming of known allergic plants, those should be suspected of being the problem. Removing a cat from the presence of particular pollens may be impossible. Another problem in the search for the offending agent is the fact that most allergies are developed to agents to which the cat has been exposed for many months or years. Therefore, it is unlikely to be to a new agent just introduced into the cat's environment. However, precipitation of an asthmatic attack may occur in response to some event: smoking in the household, something sprayed into the air (hairspray, perfume, air freshener), or a stress (overactive play with another pet or a member of the family).

It is often recommended that dusty kitty litter be replaced with another, less-dusty brand. This is an exercise worth doing, but it is not often the answer. It is probably best to avoid litters which have fresheners or deodorizers. It also might be helpful to switch from a clay-based litter to the clumping litter.

The cornerstone of treatment is steroids. These drugs block the allergic reaction and generally give relief within 30 minutes to several hours. In some cats, an injection of a long-acting steroid may last for several weeks. This is a desirable way of treating asthmatic cats that have seasonal problems. Other cats respond better to steroid tablets, especially if more prolonged treatment is needed.

Since the asthmatic's lungs are easily infected, the use of antibiotics may be necessary at certain times, usually for a period of 1 - 2 weeks.

Cats needing continuous treatment may do well with certain bronchodilators. These drugs relax the airways and allow the cat to breathe with less effort. Sometimes, a trial and error approach will be necessary to determine the best way to treat each patient.

What should I do if my cat does not respond to the prescribed treatment?

Lack of response is disappointing, but can be very meaningful. It will either cause us to try another appropriate treatment or to consider diseases which may resemble asthma. If a significant improvement does not occur within 48 hours, the cat should be re-evaluated by the veterinarian.

 ## BREEDING CATS AND RAISING KITTENS

Breeding cats and raising kittens can be an extremely rewarding experience or it may produce frustration and failure. The following information is provided in order to increase your chance of success.

How often does a female cat come into heat?

The female cat (queen) comes into heat (estrus) many times each year. The heat period lasts about 2 - 3 weeks. If she is not bred, she will return to heat in 1 - 2 weeks. This cycle will continue for several heat cycles or until she is bred. The period of time that she is out of heat will vary depending on geographic and environmental factors, such as temperature and the number of daylight hours.

What are the signs of heat?

The signs of heat are different in cats as compared to dogs. Cats have minimal vaginal bleeding, usually not even enough to be detected. Their behavior is the most notable sign. Cats become very affectionate. They rub against their owners and furniture and constantly want attention. They roll on the floor. When stroked over the back, they raise their rear quarters into the air and tread with the back legs. They also become very vocal. These behavior changes are often of concern for owners and may be interpreted as some unusual illness. In addition, queens in heat attract un-neutered male cats. Tom cats that have never been seen will appear and attempt to enter the house to get to the female.

What should I do to be sure that a breeding is accomplished successfully?

Male cats are more successful breeders in familiar surroundings. Therefore, it is preferable to take the female to the male's home for breeding. The timing for breeding cats is not highly critical or complicated because cats are induced ovulators. This means that the act of breeding stimulates the ovaries to release eggs. Therefore, the female's eggs should be released from the ovaries when the sperm are deposited in the reproductive tract at breeding. Most female cats require 3 - 4 breedings within a 24 hour period for ovulation to occur. If you haven't watched cats mating before you may be surprised. Not only do they make a lot of noise but both the tom and the queen appear to be very aggressive to each other. The male often bites the females neck during coitus. Immediately after mating the female will usually roll on the floor. Do not worry, these behaviors are completely normal and part of the process to encourage ovulation to occur. Once ovulation has occurred, the female cat will go out of heat within a day or two.

What should I expect during pregnancy?

Pregnancy, also called the gestation period, ranges from 60 to 67 days and averages 63 days; most cats deliver (queen) between days 63 and 65. The only way to accurately determine the stage of pregnancy is to count days from the time of breeding. If possible, the breeding date(s) should be recorded. The mother should be examined by a veterinarian 3 weeks after breeding to confirm her pregnancy.

A pregnant cat should be fed a kitten formulation of a premium brand of cat food for the duration of the pregnancy and through the nursing period. These diets are generally available through veterinary hospitals or pet stores. Kitten diets provide all the extra nutrition needed for the mother and her litter. If the mother is eating one of these diets, no calcium, vitamin, or mineral supplements are needed. (The kitten formulation is necessary to provide the extra nutrients for pregnancy and nursing.)

During pregnancy the mother's food consumption will often reach 1.5 times her level before pregnancy. By the end of the nursing period, it may exceed 2 times the pre-pregnancy amount. Do not withhold food; increasing the number of feedings per day is helpful in allowing her to eat enough for her needs and those of the kittens.

What should I do to prepare for queening?

From the time of breeding, many cats show behavioral changes. Most develop an unusually sweet and loving disposition and demand more affection and attention. However, some may become uncharacteristically irritable. Some experience a few days of vomiting ("morning sickness") followed by the development of a ravenous appetite which persists throughout the pregnancy.

During the latter stages of pregnancy, the expectant mother begins to look for a secure place for delivery. Many become uncomfortable being alone and will cling closely to their owner. At the onset of labor, many nervously seek a place to make the "nest" or birthing place. If the cat is attached to her owner, she will not want to be left alone at the time of delivery. If left alone, she may delay delivery until the owner returns.

Prior to the time of delivery, a queening box should be selected and placed in a secluded place, such as a closet or a dark corner. The box should be large enough for the cat to move around freely, but have low enough sides so that she can see out and so you can reach inside to give assistance, if needed. The bottom of the box should be lined with several layers of newspapers. These provide a private hiding place for the expectant and delivering mother and will absorb the birthing fluids. The upper, soiled layers may be removed with minimal interruption to the mother and her newborn kittens.

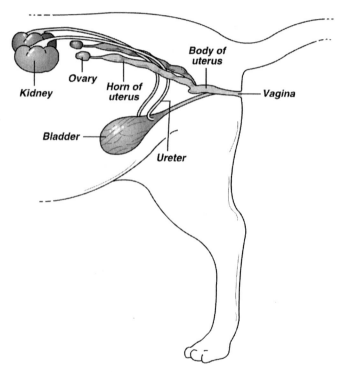

Diagram of reproductive organs and urinary tract of the female cat.

What happens during labor and delivery?

Most cats experience delivery without complications; however, first-time mothers should be attended by their owners until at least one or two kittens are born. If these are born quickly and without assistance, further attendance may not be necessary, although it is desirable. If the owner elects to leave, care should be taken so that the cat does not try to follow and leave the queening box.

The signs of impending labor generally include nervousness and panting. The cat will often stop eating during the last 24 hours before labor. She will also usually have a drop in rectal temperature below 100°F (37.8°C). The temperature drop may occur intermittently for several days prior to delivery, but it will usually be constant for the last 24 hours.

Delivery times will vary. Shorthair cats and cats having slim heads, such as Siamese, may complete delivery in one to two hours. Domestic body type cats (having large, round heads) generally require longer delivery times. Persian kittens and kittens from cats of similar body type tend to be very large and have sizable heads that make delivery more difficult. It is not unusual for Persians to rest an hour or more between each kitten. Rarely, a cat may deliver one or two kittens then have labor stop for as long as twenty-four hours before the remainder of the litter is born. However, if labor does not resume within a few hours after the delivery of the first kittens, examination by a veterinarian is advised. If labor is interrupted for twenty-four hours or more, veterinary assistance should definitely be obtained.

Kittens are usually born head first; however, breech presentations, in which the kitten is delivered tail-end first, occur about 40% of the time and are also considered normal. Each kitten is enclosed in a sac that is part of the placenta ("afterbirth"). The placentas usually pass after the kittens are born. However, any that do not pass will disintegrate and pass within 24 - 48 hours after delivery. It is normal for the mother to eat the placentas.

If the delivery proceeds normally, a few contractions will discharge the kitten; it should exit the birth canal within ten minutes of being visible. Following delivery, the mother should lick the newborn's face. She will then proceed to wash it and toss it about. Her tongue is used to tear the sac and expose the mouth and nose. This vigorous washing stimulates circulation, causing the kitten to cry and begin breathing; it also dries the newborn's haircoat. The mother will sever the umbilical cord by chewing it about 3/4 to 1 inch (1.9 to 2.5 cm) from the body. Next, she will eat the placenta.

If the kitten or a fluid-filled bubble is partially visible from the vagina but birth is not progressing, the owner should assist delivery. A dampened gauze or thin wash cloth can be used to break the bubble and grasp the head or feet. When a contraction occurs, firm traction should be applied in a downward (i.e., toward her rear feet) direction. If reasonable traction is applied without being able to remove the kitten, or if the queen cries intensely during this process, the kitten is probably lodged. A veterinarian's assistance should be sought without delay.

It is normal for the female to remove the placental sac and clean the kittens; however, first-time mothers may be bewildered by the experience and hesitate to do so. If the sac is not removed within a few minutes after delivery, the kitten will suffocate, so you should be prepared to intervene. The kitten's face should be wiped with a damp wash cloth or gauze to remove the sac and allow breathing. Vigorous rubbing with a soft, warm towel will stimulate circulation and dry the hair. The umbilical cord should be tied with cord (i.e., sewing thread, dental floss) and cut with clean scissors. The cord should be tied snugly to the kitten's body and cut about 1/2 inch (1.3 cm) from the body so it is unlikely to be pulled off as the kitten moves around the queening box.

Newborn kittens may aspirate fluid into the lungs, as evidenced by a raspy noise during respiration. This fluid can be removed by the following procedure. First, the kitten should be held in the palm of your hand. The kitten's face should be cradled between the first two fingers. The head should be held firmly with this hand, and the body should be held firmly with the other. Next, a downward swing motion with the hands should make the kitten gasp. Gravity will help the fluid and mucus to flow out of the lungs. This process may be tried several times until the lungs sound clear. The tongue is a reliable indicator of successful respiration. If the kitten is getting adequate oxygen, it will appear pink to red. A bluish colored tongue indicates insufficient oxygen to the lungs, signaling that the swinging procedure should be repeated.

It may be helpful to have a smaller, clean, dry box lined with a warm towel for the newborn kittens. (A towel can be warmed in a microwave oven.) After the kitten is stable and the cord has been tied, it should be placed in the incubator box while the mother is completing delivery. Warmth is essential so a heating pad or hot water bottle may be placed in the box, or a heat lamp may be placed nearby. If a heating pad is used, it should be placed on the low setting and covered with a towel to prevent overheating. A hot water bottle should be covered with a towel. Remember, the newborn kittens may be unable to move away from the heat source. Likewise, caution should also be exercised when using a heat lamp.

Once delivery is completed, the soiled newspapers should be removed from the whelping or queening box. The box should be lined with soft bedding prior to the kittens' return. The mother should accept the kittens readily and recline for nursing.

The mother and her litter should be examined by a veterinarian within 24 hours after the delivery is completed. This visit is to check the mother for complete delivery, and to check the newborn kittens. The mother may receive an injection to contract the uterus and stimulate milk production.

The mother will have a bloody vaginal discharge for 3 - 7 days following delivery. If it continues for longer than one week, she should be examined by a veterinarian for possible problems.

What happens if my cat has trouble delivering her kittens?

Although most cats deliver without need for assistance, problems do arise which require the attention of a veterinarian. Professional assistance should be sought if any of the following occur:

1) Twenty minutes of intense labor occurs without a kitten being delivered.

2) Ten minutes of intense labor occurs when a kitten or a fluid-filled bubble is visible in the birth canal and gentle pulling on the fetus (*see above*) does not help or induces pain in the mother.

3) The mother experiences sudden depression or marked lethargy.

4) The mother's body temperature exceeds 103°F (39.4°C) (via a rectal thermometer).

5) Fresh blood discharges from the vagina for more than 10 minutes.

Difficulty delivering (dystocia) may be managed with or without surgery. The condition of the mother, size of the litter, and size of the kittens are factors used in making that decision.

Is premature delivery a likely problem?

Occasionally, a mother will deliver a litter several days premature. The kittens may be small, thin, and have little or no hair. It is possible for them to survive, but they require an enormous amount of care, since they are subject to chilling and are frequently very weak and unable to swallow. Some may be able to nurse but are so weak that they must be held next to the mother. Kittens that do not nurse can be fed with a small syringe, bottle, or stomach tube. The equipment and instructions for these procedures are available from a veterinarian. Premature kittens must be kept warm.

The mother can provide sufficient radiant heat from her body if she will stay close to them. If she refuses, heat can be provided with a heat lamp, heating pad, or hot water bottle. Excessive heat can be just as harmful as chilling, so any form of artificial heat must be controlled. The temperature in the box should be maintained at 85 - 90°F (29.4 - 32.2°C), but the box should be large enough so the kittens can move away from the heat if it becomes uncomfortable.

Is it likely that one or more kittens will be stillborn?

It is not uncommon for one or two kittens in a litter to be stillborn. Sometimes, a stillborn kitten will disrupt labor, resulting in dystocia. At other times the dead kitten will be born normally. Very occasionally, one or more of the kittens may have died at an earlier stage in the pregnancy. These kittens dry-out in the womb and appear as semi-preserved fetuses at birth. For this reason, they are sometimes called "mummies". Although there is always a cause for this occurrence, it is often not easily determined without an autopsy that includes cultures and the submission of tissues to a pathologist. This is only recommended in special circumstances.

What do I do to care for the newborn kittens?

The mother will spend most of her time with the kittens during the next few days. The kittens need to be kept warm and to nurse frequently; they should be checked every few hours to make certain that they are warm and well fed. The mother should be checked to make certain that she is producing adequate milk.

If the mother does not stay in the box, the kittens' temperature must be monitored. If the kittens are cold, supplemental heating should be provided. During the first four days of life, the newborns' box should be maintained at 85 - 90°F (29.4 - 32.2°C). The temperature may gradually be decreased to 80°F (26.7°C) by the seventh to tenth day and to 72°F (22.2°C) by the end of the fourth week. If the litter is large, the temperature need not be as high. As kittens huddle together, their body heat provides additional warmth.

If the mother feels the kittens are in danger or if there is too much light, she may become anxious. Placing a sheet or cloth over most of the top of the box to obscure much of the light may resolve the problem. An enclosed box is also a solution. Some cats, especially first-time mothers, are more anxious than others. Such cats may attempt to hide their young, even from her owner. Moving from place to place may continue and will endanger the kittens if they are placed in a cold or drafty location. Cats with this behavior should be caged in a secluded area. This type of mother has also been known to kill her kittens as a means of "protecting" them from danger.

What are the signs that the kittens are not doing well and what do I do?

Kittens should eat or sleep 90% of the time during the first 2 weeks. If they are crying during or after eating, they are usually becoming ill or are not getting adequate milk. A newborn kitten is very susceptible to infections and can die within 24 hours. If excessive crying occurs, the mother and entire litter should be examined by a veterinarian promptly.

When the milk supply is inadequate, supplemental feeding one to three times per day is recommended and should be performed on any litter with 5+ kittens. There are several commercial formulae available that are made to supply the needs of kittens. They require no preparation other than warming. They should be warmed to 95 - 100°F (35 - 37.8°C) before feeding. Its temperature can be tested on one's forearm; it should be about the same as one's skin. An alternative is canned goats' milk that is available in most grocery stores. The commercial products have directions concerning feeding amounts. If the kittens are still nursing from their mother, the amounts recommended will be excessive. Generally, 1/3 to 1/2 of the listed amount should be the daily goal. Supplemental feeding may be continued until the kittens are old enough to eat kitten food.

If the mother does not produce milk or her milk becomes infected, the kittens will also cry. If this occurs, the entire litter could die within 24 to 48 hours. Total replacement feeding, using the mentioned products, or adopting the kittens to another nursing mother is usually necessary. If replacement feeding is chosen, the amounts of milk listed on the product should be fed. Kittens less than 2 weeks of age should be fed every 3 - 4 hours. Kittens 2 - 4 weeks of age do well with feedings every 6 - 8 hours. Weaning, as described below, should begin at 3 - 4 weeks of age.

What should I expect during the kittens' first few weeks of life?

For the first month of life kittens require very little care from the owner because their mother will feed and care for them. They are born with their eyes closed, but they will open in 7 to 14 days. If swelling or bulging is noted under the eyelids, they should be opened gently. A cotton ball dampened with warm water may be used to assist opening the lids. If the swelling is due to infection, pus will exit the open eyelids and should be treated as prescribed by a veterinarian. If the eyes have not opened within 14 days of age, they should be opened by a veterinarian.

Kittens should be observed for their rate of growth. They should double their birth weight in about one week.

At two weeks of age, kittens should be alert and trying to stand. At three weeks, they generally try to climb out of their box. At four weeks, all of the kittens should be able to walk, run, and play.

Kittens should begin eating solid food about 3 1/2 to 4 1/2 weeks of age. Initially, one of the milk replacers or cow's milk diluted 50:50 with water should be placed in a flat saucer. The kittens' noses should be dipped into the milk 2 or 3 times per day until they begin to lap; this usually takes 1 - 3 days. Next, canned kitten food should be placed in the milk until it is soggy. As the kittens lap the milk, they will also ingest the food. The amount of milk should be decreased daily until they are eating the canned food with little or no moisture added; this should occur by 4 to 6 weeks of age.

I have heard of milk fever. What exactly is it?

Eclampsia or milk fever is a depletion of calcium from the mother due to heavy milk production. It generally occurs when the kittens are 3 - 5 weeks old (just before weaning) and most often to mothers with large litters. The mother has muscle spasms resulting in rigid legs, spastic movements, and heavy panting. This can be fatal in 30 - 60 minutes, so a veterinarian should be consulted immediately.

Do kittens need a special diet?

Diet is extremely important for a growing kitten. There are many commercial foods specially formulated for kittens. These foods meet their unique nutritional requirements and should be fed until 12 months of age. Kitten foods are available in dry and canned formulations. Dry foods are less expensive and can be left in the bowl for the kitten to eat at will. Kittens will eat small amounts as often as 12 times during the day. Canned foods offer a change and are just as nutritious.

We recommend that you buy FOOD FORMULATED FOR KITTENS. Adult formulations are not recommended since they do not provide the nutrition required for a kitten. Advertisements tend to promote taste rather than nutrition so one should be careful that their influence on purchasing habits is not detrimental to one's cat. Generic foods should be avoided. Table food is not recommended; although often more appealing than cat food, balanced, complete nutrition is usually compromised. Dog food should not be fed to cats since it is deficient in vital nutrients and in the amount of protein required by kittens and adult cats.

We recommend that you buy NAME BRAND FOOD. It is generally a good idea to avoid generic brands of food. We recommend that you only buy food which has the AAFCO (American Association of Feed Control Officials) certification. Usually, you can find this information very easily on the food label. AAFCO is an organization which oversees the entire pet food industry. It does not endorse any particular food, but it will tell you if the food has met the minimum requirements for nutrition which are set by the industry. Most commercial pet foods will have the AAFCO label. In Canada look for foods approved by the Canadian Veterinary Medical Association (CVMA).

When should vaccinations begin?

Kittens are provided some immunity to feline diseases before and shortly after birth. Some of the mother's antibodies cross the placenta and enter the kittens' circulation. Most maternal antibodies are provided in the mother's milk, particularly in the first milk or colostrum. They are absorbed from the kitten's stomach and intestine into the blood stream. These "maternal antibodies" protect the kittens against the diseases to which the mother is immune. This explains why it is desirable to booster the mother's vaccinations within a few months prior to breeding.

Although very protective, maternal antibodies last for only a few weeks; after this time, the kitten becomes susceptible to disease. The vaccination program should be started at about 6 to 8 weeks of age. Kittens should be vaccinated against feline enteritis (distemper), respiratory organisms (rhinotracheitis, calici, and pneumonitis), and rabies. If the kitten will be allowed to go outdoors or will be in contact with cats that go outdoors, leukemia and feline infectious peritonitis (FIP) vaccine should also be considered. Your cat's needs will be discussed at the time of the first visit for vaccinations.

Maternal antibodies are passed in the mother's milk only during the first 1 - 3 days after delivery. If, for any reason, the kittens do not nurse during this important period of time, their vaccinations should begin about 2 to 4 weeks of age, depending on likely disease exposure. A veterinarian can make specific recommendations for each particular situation.

Do all kittens have worms?

Intestinal parasites ("worms") are common in kittens. Symptoms include general poor condition, chronic soft or bloody stools, loss of appetite, a pot-bellied appearance, loss of luster of the haircoat, and weight loss. Some parasites are transmitted from the mother to her offspring and others are carried by fleas. Some are transmitted through the stool of an infected cat. Very few of these parasites are visible in the stool, so their eggs must be detected by the veterinarian with a microscope.

A microscopic examination of the feces will reveal the eggs of most of these parasites. Generally this test should be performed at the time of the first vaccinations. However, it may be performed as early as 3 weeks of age if a parasite problem is suspected. Treatment is based on the type of parasites found although some veterinarians elect to treat all kittens because they know that fecal tests can be falsely negative. Your veterinarian should be consulted for specific recommendations for your kittens.

 CARDIOMYOPATHY

What is cardiomyopathy?

Literally, the term "cardiomyopathy" means disease of the heart muscle. More specifically, cardiomyopathy (CM) is a disease of the heart muscle in which either the heart walls thicken greatly (hypertrophic and restrictive forms) or stretch greatly (dilated form). In either form, the heart's function is greatly compromised leading to an eventual state of heart failure.

What causes cardiomyopathy?

There have been several causes of CM identified. A deficiency of taurine, an essential amino acid, will cause dilated CM. Taurine was deficient in many commercial cat foods until its deficiency was identified; however, cat foods are now properly supplemented. Hyperthyroidism, a non-cancerous growth of the thyroid gland, can cause a variation of the hypertrophic form. The restrictive form is associated with an unidentified inflammatory process within the heart muscle. However, many cases of CM are not caused by any of these processes, and we do not understand their origin.

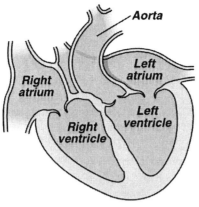

Normal heart

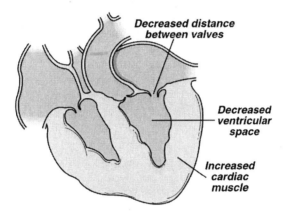

Hypertrophic cardiomyopathy

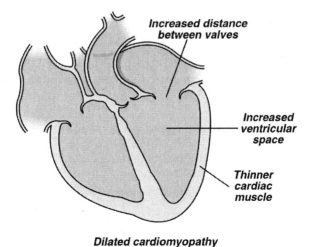

Dilated cardiomyopathy

What does a cat with cardiomyopathy look like?

Cardiomyopathy is a disease that usually takes several weeks to months to progress to a serious stage. During the early weeks of the disease, the cat will probably look normal. Cats have the ability to hide serious illness until it reaches a crisis stage. Therefore, most cats that develop clinical signs of cardiomyopathy will appear to have been ill for only a few days. A few days of inactivity and poor appetite occur first. Just prior to the state of heart failure and death, the cat may become very inactive and exhibit labored breathing. Both may be due to insufficient oxygen transport to the body's tissues; the latter may also be due to a collection of fluid in or around the lungs.

How is this disease diagnosed?

Diagnosis is generally made with a chest radiograph (x-ray). The heart will have an abnormal shape and fluid may be detected in or around the lungs. If a large amount of fluid is present around the lungs, it may be necessary to remove it and take more radiographs because the presence of this fluid interferes with evaluation of the heart. Many cases also require better visualization of the heart with an echocardiogram, or sonogram. This is a non-invasive method of looking at the heart while it is pumping. Sound waves are used to make this dynamic study of the heart. Radiographs can tell us about the size and shape of the heart but nothing about heart function. Ultrasound can provide this information. Ultrasound will also allow measurement of the heart muscle to determine if it is too thick (hypertrophic or restrictive CM) or too thin (dilated CM). Finally, an electrocardiogram (EKG) is useful to evaluate the rhythm of the heart.

Determination of the level of thyroid hormone (T_4) in the blood is often indicated in evaluating cats with hypertrophic CM. This simple blood test can help identify an overactive thyroid gland as the underlying cause of the heart disease.

What is involved with treatment?

Treatment is based on the type of CM present. Different drugs are used for the different forms. Therefore, if at all possible, tests necessary to define the specific forms are performed before treatment begins. Fortunately, most of these cats can be stabilized with the correct drug; however, continual medication may be necessary since the disease cannot be cured. The exception to this is the cat with hyperthyroidism that is causing CM. This form of CM is potentially reversible if the cat receives appropriate and timely treatment for the thyroid disease.

Are there complications that may occur?

Most of the cats with cardiomyopathy develop signs of heart failure as previously described. However, cats with CM are prone to producing blood clots within their hearts. When these clots escape the heart, they travel through various arteries leading from the heart. They eventually lodge in a narrow part of the artery. The most common site for clots to lodge is the point at which the aorta splits before going into the rear legs. Thus, these cats often become paralyzed very suddenly and are in significant pain. In many cases, it is paralysis and pain that first becomes noticeable and is the reason that medical treatment is sought. This may be mistaken for an uncomplicated lameness or even a broken leg. Within a few minutes to hours, there are no pulses in one or both rear legs, the legs are cold, and the foot-pads appear blue due to the lack of oxygen.

Treatment of the paralyzed cat concentrates on drugs to relieve pain and to hasten the return of circulation to the legs. Since these cats also have severe heart disease, they make poor surgical candidates. Therefore, surgery to remove the clot is not advisable due to the high incidence of death during surgery.

The prognosis for the paralyzed cat is variable, but it is improved if the cat receives immediate attention. Within 3 - 10 days, circulation is generally restored, and leg function returns in most cats. However, the heart disease must be controlled quickly or they will die.

What is the prognosis for cats with cardiomyopathy?

The prognosis for CM is variable depending on the form of the disease and the severity at the time of diagnosis. Many cats will live up to 3 years if properly medicated, but the survival rate averages about 6 months. The exception is when CM is caused by hyperthyroidism. If hyperthyroidism is successfully treated, the heart function will generally return to normal and the cat will no longer require treatment.

CAT SCRATCH DISEASE

What is Cat Scratch Disease and what causes it?

Cat Scratch Disease (CSD) is also known as Cat Scratch Fever. It is a disease of humans, not of cats. However, a cat scratch is generally associated with it. The cause of CSD has recently been identified as a bacteria-like organism called *Bartonella henselaea*. Most cases are reported in the fall and winter, but the cause for this seasonality is unknown.

How common is this disease?

Antibodies are proteins which are produced by the immune system in response to some stimulus. About 5% of the United States population has antibodies to CSD. Interestingly, about 20% of U.S. veterinarians also have CSD antibodies. However, very few of those testing positive have actually had the disease. The majority have had infections which have not been apparent or have been exposed to the CSD organism without any signs of disease.

This is generally a mild disease in humans. Many people experience only fever, chills, and lethargy that last a few days. Unless the skin test is performed or the organism is cultured, it may be diagnosed as influenza. However, the more severe forms of the disease will produce very high fevers, marked lethargy, anorexia, and swollen lymph nodes, usually in the arm-pits or groin. Rarely, the lymph nodes may enlarge to the point of rupturing or they may need to be opened surgically to establish drainage and relieve pain.

The disease is self-limiting. It runs a course of several days to several weeks and then subsides. Now that the causative organism has been identified, most cases can be treated quite successfully with appropriate antibiotics.

The cat is involved because most cases of CSD are preceded by a cat scratch. Our best understanding of the cat's involvement is as follows:

- The cat is almost always a kitten; adults are rarely involved.
- The cat appears to be contagious for only about 2 - 3 weeks.
- The contact is by a scratch and not a bite, although the organism lives in the cat's mouth. It is transmitted to the claws by licking. Declawing the cat may not necessarily prevent transmission although it will help.
- The cat can be tested for the organism (a blood test) and treated with antibiotics. However, reinfection can occur.

One should be concerned about a family member having CSD. However, banning cats indefinitely from the household is not warranted. It has been shown that less than 10% of family members scratched by the same cat develop the disease. In addition, there has not been a person recorded as having had the disease twice.

 CESAREAN SECTION POST-OPERATIVE INSTRUCTION

A cesarean section is major surgery to remove kittens from the uterus. Most cats recover quickly from this procedure; however, if your cat was in labor for several hours before surgery was performed, her recovery will be slower, and she will need extra attention and help with her litter.

What should I expect during the mother's recovery period?

The mother has been given an anesthetic that is eliminated from her body rather quickly. Most cats are raising their heads about the time they arrive at home. Complete recovery from anesthetic may take 2 - 6 hours, depending on her physical condition at the time of surgery and her age. During the recovery period, she must be restrained in such a way that she does not fall and hurt herself or roll over and crush the kittens. The kittens should not be left alone with her until she is completely awake and coordinated.

The mother should be interested in eating within a few hours after she is completely awake. Allow her to eat and drink all that she wants, being careful that she does not overload her stomach. This can result in vomiting. Her food intake at this time should be about one and a half times her food intake before she became pregnant. By the third or fourth week of nursing, her food intake may be twice or even two and a half times normal. The mother's temperature may rise 1 - 2°F (0.5 - 1°C) above normal for the first 1 - 3 days, then it should return to the normal range. The normal range is 100 - 102°F (37.8 - 38.9°C). If the mother's temperature goes above 104°F (40°C), **she and her litter** should be examined by a veterinarian for the presence of serious complications.

Caution:A CAT SHOULD NEVER BE GIVEN ACETAMINOPHEN and aspirin should only be given on the directions of a veterinarian.

When should the kittens begin to nurse?

The kittens should be ready to nurse as soon as you arrive at home. Although the mother will not be awake enough to handle the nursing alone, it is still possible for you to assist the process by making her lie still so the kittens can nurse. If the mother does not have any milk at first, you may supplement the kittens for the first day or two. There are several good commercial feline milk replacers available. Nursing bottles are available, made in the appropriate size for tiny mouths. The following formula may be used for a day or two if the other products are not available:

> 1 cup (240 mL) milk + 1 tablespoon (15 mL) corn oil +
> 1 pinch of salt + 3 egg yolks (no whites). Blend
> together until uniform. It should be fed at the rate of
> 1 oz (30 cc or 30 mL) per 1/4 lb of kitten weight PER
> 24 HOURS. That amount should be divided into 3 - 5
> feedings. The average newborn kitten weighs 1/4 lb
> (100 g) at birth.

Another alternative is canned goat's milk that is available in most grocery stores. It should be fed at the above amounts. Although we prefer that kittens begin nursing immediately, a healthy newborn can survive nicely for up to 12 hours without nursing. However, if the newborn is weak, dehydrated, or chilled, nourishment must be given very soon.

How warm should we keep the room where the kittens are?

A newborn kitten is not able to regulate its body temperature very well. As long as the kittens stay near their mother, the room temperature is not too critical. However, if they are not with their mother, the room temperature should be between 85 and 90°F (29.4 - 32.2°C). If the litter is kept outside, chilling or overheating is much more likely to occur. The newborns should be kept inside the house or the garage, if possible.

Is a bloody vaginal discharge normal?

A bloody vaginal discharge is normal for 3 - 7 days following birth. It may be quite heavy for the first 1 - 3 days, then it should begin to diminish. If it continues for longer than one week, she should be checked for the presence of infection. If she was spayed at the time of the surgery, there should be no vaginal discharge.

What does it mean if the kittens are crying frequently?

Kittens should sleep or be nursing 90% of the time. If they are crying or whining, something is likely to be wrong. Uterine infections, inadequate milk, poor-quality milk, and infected milk are the most likely causes. The entire litter can die within 24 hours if one of these occurs. If you are not comfortable with the way the litter is doing, the kittens and the mother should be examined by a veterinarian.

When are her stitches removed?

The stitches may or may not need to be removed, depending on the type of suture material used. As a general rule, if the stitches are visible, they will have to be removed. Removal should occur at 10 - 14 days after surgery.

When should the kittens be weaned?

Weaning should begin when the kittens are about 3 1/2 weeks old. The first step is to place a 50:50 mixture of water and cow's milk in a flat saucer. The kittens' noses should be dipped in this mixture 2 - 3 times per day until they begin to lap. Once lapping begins, a kitten-type canned food should be crumbled in the water:milk mixture. As they begin to eat the solid food, the water:milk mixture should be reduced until they are eating only the solid food. Once they are eating solid food (about 5 - 6 weeks of age), they may be placed in their new home.

When are the kittens treated for worms?

Kittens can be treated for worms when they are 3 **and** 6 weeks of age. It is important that accurate weights are obtained for the kittens so that the proper dose of medication can be used.

When should vaccinations begin?

First vaccinations typically begin at 6 - 8 weeks of age. If your kittens were not able to nurse during the first 3 days of life, they will not have received proper immunity from their mother. In this situation, vaccinations should begin about 2 weeks of age.

 CHYLOTHORAX

What is chylothorax?

Chylothorax is a disorder characterized by the accumulation of fluid in the pleural space. This space is located between the lungs and the chest wall. This disorder differs from other fluid-causing diseases because the unique fluid that collects (chyle) is produced only by the lymphatic system.

The body has three vessel systems. The arteries and the veins are two of these. The third vessel system is composed of the lymphatics; these vessels carry lymph from the lymph nodes into a major vein near the heart.

As fluid accumulates in the chest cavity, the cat tries to compensate by breathing more rapidly. Because the pleural space is full of chyle, the lungs are unable to fully expand. Pain in the chest cavity may also contribute to shallow breathing. The inability to breathe deeply is extremely stressful for the cat and may lead to respiratory failure and death.

What causes chylothorax?

At present, two main processes are known to lead to chylothorax. The first of these, a ruptured thoracic duct, may occur with traumatic events, such as automobile accidents or falls from buildings. The second disease mechanism, increased pressure within the thoracic duct, has been associated with heart failure, heartworms, and tumors within the chest. In many cats, identification of the exact cause remains elusive; these cases are called "idiopathic."

What are the signs of chylothorax?

There are many different causes of respiratory distress in cats. There are no clinical signs unique to chylothorax which would allow us to diagnose it on physical examination alone. Difficulty breathing and a rapid heart rate are commonly reported; coughing is noted in some cats. Sometimes, the clinical signs may be produced by the underlying disease process.

How is chylothorax diagnosed?

We begin with a chest radiograph (x-ray). This will confirm the presence of fluid in the pleural space. A sample of this fluid is removed from the chest for a series of tests. The first test is visual inspection. Chylous fluid is milky white in color, though there is sometimes a slight red (blood) tinge. Chemical tests will reveal a high level of triglycerides (fat) and cells typical of lymphatic fluid.

Once the presence of chylothorax is confirmed, it is important to look for an underlying disease. Further blood tests, chest and abdominal radiographs, cardiac tests, and a heartworm test are included in the search.

What is the treatment?

The first phase of treatment is to relieve breathing difficulty. Initially, fluid will be drained with a syringe and needle. In almost all cases, the fluid will reform unless a drain tube is surgically implanted to facilitate daily drainage. The drain tube is left in the chest until chyle accumulation stops. If this does not happen within 1 - 2 weeks, exploratory chest surgery may be recommended to look for an underlying cause or to repair a torn thoracic duct that will not heal on its own.

Because chyle contains a large amount of fat, a low-fat diet may be beneficial in reducing chyle production.

If an underlying cause is found, specific treatment for that disorder is also begun.

Can chylothorax be a recurring problem?

Yes. If there is an underlying disease that cannot be identified or cured, chylothorax may recur. The cat should be observed closely for signs of breathing difficulties; this may occur in a few days to a few months. In certain circumstances, the cat may be referred to a veterinary surgical specialist for placement of a special shunt, or drain. This procedure allows the chyle to flow from the chest into the abdominal cavity. The results of the surgery are variable and management of the shunt tube can be quite frustrating.

What is the prognosis for a cat with chylothorax?

The prognosis is generally good if three things occur:

- *The cat must be stabilized so that it can breathe better.* Chylothorax severely compromises respiration. The stress of testing and surgically placing the chest drain tube can be enough to cause death if the cat's condition is very serious.

- *The underlying disease must be cured.* Your veterinarian would like to identify the underlying problem, but some causes are self-limiting. If this is the case, it may resolve even if it is not diagnosed.

- *The cat must be treated before complications occur.* Chyle is irritating to the chest wall and to the outer surface of the lungs. If it is present for several weeks, permanent adhesions and scarring will occur. This is called fibrosing pleuritis; once it develops, the cat has a guarded prognosis for full recovery, regardless of the underlying cause.

 COCCIDIOSIS

What is coccidiosis?

Coccidiosis is an infection with a one-celled organism; these organisms are classified as protozoa and are called coccidia. Coccidia are not worms; they are microscopic parasites which live within cells of the intestinal lining. Because they live in the intestinal tract and commonly cause diarrhea, they are often confused with worms.

How did my cat become infected with coccidia?

Oocysts (immature coccidia) are passed in the stool of the cat. They lie in the environment and eventually sporulate (mature) into a more developed oocyst which can infect the cat again. Other cats, dogs, or mice may also become infected. This process can occur in as little as 6 hours, but it usually takes 7 - 10 days. If the sporulated oocysts are swallowed, they mature in the cat's intestine to complete the life cycle. If the oocysts should be swallowed by a mouse, the cat may also become infected by eating the mouse.

What kinds of problems are caused by coccidial infection?

Most cats that are infected with coccidia do not have diarrhea or any other clinical signs. When the eggs (oocysts) are found in the stool of a cat without diarrhea, they are generally considered a transient, insignificant finding. However, in kittens and debilitated adult cats, they may cause severe, watery diarrhea, dehydration, abdominal distress, and vomiting. In severe cases, death may occur.

How is coccidial infection diagnosed?

Coccidiosis is diagnosed by performing a microscopic examination of a stool sample. Since the oocysts are much smaller than the eggs of the intestinal worms, a very careful study must be made. Infection with some of the less common coccidial parasites is diagnosed with a blood test.

How is the coccidial infection treated?

The most common drug used to eliminate coccidia is a sulfa-type antibiotic. It is given for 10 - 14 days. Other drugs are also used if diarrhea and dehydration occur. If the sulfa-type drug is not effective, others are available.

Reinfection of cats is common so environmental disinfection is important. The use of chlorine bleach, one cup in a gallon (500 ml in 4 liters) of water, is effective if the surfaces and premises can be safely treated with it.

Are the coccidial parasites of my cat infectious to humans?

The most common coccidia found in cats do not have any affect on humans. However, less common types of coccidia are potentially infectious to humans.

One parasite, called *Cryptosporidium*, may be carried by cats or dogs and may be transmitted to people. This parasite has also been found in public water supplies in some major cites.

Another coccidial organism, *Toxoplasma*, is of particular concern to pregnant women because of the potential to cause birth defects in newborns.

These two coccidial parasites pose a health risk for immuno-suppressed humans (i.e., AIDS patients, those taking immune suppressing drugs, cancer patients, the elderly). Good hygiene and proper disposal of cat feces are important in minimizing risk of transmission of all feline parasites to humans. Although there is risk of the cat transmitting these two particular parasites to humans, it does not warrant removing the cat from the household except in very rare instances.

I know that knee injuries are common in people. Do they occur in cats?

The knee joint of the cat is one of the weakest in the body. Just as football players frequently suffer knee injuries, the cat also has knee injuries.

Why is the knee so likely to be injured?

The knee joint is relatively unstable because there is no interlocking of bones in the joint. Instead, the two main bones, the femur and tibia, are joined with several ligaments. When severe twisting of the joint occurs, the most common injury is a rupture of the anterior cruciate ligament. When it is torn, an instability occurs that allows the bones to move in an abnormal fashion in relation to each other. It is not really possible to bear weight on the leg.

How is it diagnosed?

The most reliable means of diagnosing this injury is to move the femur and tibia in a certain way to demonstrate the instability. This movement is called a "drawer sign." It can usually be demonstrated with the cat awake, but if the cat is in pain or is uncooperative, examining the knee under sedation may be necessary.

How is it treated?

The proper means of solving this problem is with surgery. A skilled surgeon can fashion a replacement ligament and stabilize the joint so that it functions normally. If surgery is not performed within a few days to a week, arthritic changes will begin that cannot be reversed even with surgery.

I have heard of torn cartilage. Does this also occur?

Occasionally the injury that causes a ruptured anterior cruciate ligament will also result in tearing of one or both of the menisci or "cartilages". At the time of surgery, these are examined and removed if necessary.

What happens if surgery is not performed?

It is not unusual for a cat that has a ruptured cruciate ligament to become sound (will no longer limp) even if surgery is not performed. This generally occurs within one month of the injury. However, arthritis will usually begin and result in lameness a few months later. That lameness cannot be corrected, therefore surgery is strongly recommended.

My cat is overweight. Does that relate to this injury?

A special note is appropriate concerning the cat's weight. Obesity or excessive weight can be a strong contributing factor in cruciate rupture. The ligament may become weakened due to carrying too much weight and thus tear easily. Obesity will make the recovery time much longer, and it will make the other knee very susceptible to cruciate rupture. If your cat has a weight problem, there are prescription diets that can be used to assist weight reduction.

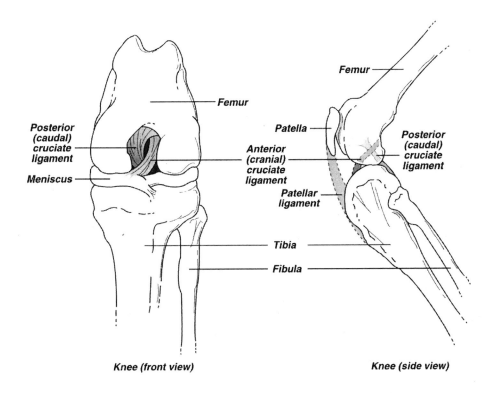

Diagram to show relationship of cruciate ligaments to the knee joint.

 CYSTITIS

What is feline cystitis?

The term "cystitis" literally means inflammation of the urinary bladder. Although this term is rather general, there is a common form of cystitis that occurs in male and female cats. This disease is also known as Feline Urologic Syndrome (FUS) or Feline Lower Urinary Tract Disease (FLUTD). It affects the bladder (not the kidneys), resulting in the production of tiny crystals and urine which is bloody. The cat often urinates much more frequently than normal, usually with the passage of only a few drops of urine. This is often confused with constipation. Many cats will urinate in places other than the litter box, and often on hard surfaces such as tile floors, counter tops, sinks, and bathtubs. They should not be punished for doing so.

What causes feline cystitis?

We are not completely sure of the cause of this problem. Bacterial infections are the most common cause of cystitis in dogs and humans, but most cats with cystitis do not have bacteria in their urine. Neutering of male cats and feeding of dry cat food have been proposed as potential causes, but these have been disproved as initiating factors. It is true, however, that many dry foods may aggravate the problem after it begins. A herpes virus has been incriminated and someday may be proven to be the cause. Despite extensive research, the cause remains elusive.

Are bloody urine and straining to urinate the main problems?

Most cats with cystitis exhibit blood in the urine and discomfort in urinating. The discomfort is usually mild but can become much worse if it is not treated. Female cats may develop 1/2 inch diameter stones in the bladder that must usually be surgically removed. Male cats may develop enough crystals in the urethra (the narrow tube carrying urine out of the body) to cause an obstruction. This obstruction prevents elimination of urine from the bladder. If the obstruction is not relieved within 48 hours, most cats will die from kidney failure and the retention of toxins that were not removed by the kidneys. Because the urethra is relatively larger in the female cat, the emergency posed by complete obstruction is almost always found in male cats.

How is cystitis treated?

Each cat with cystitis is treated according to the changes in the urine (pH, crystals, blood, etc.), the type of crystals present, the presenting clinical signs (straining, increased frequency, etc.), and the presence or absence of a bladder stone or urethral obstruction.

If neither a bladder stone nor urethral obstruction is present, proper medication will generally relieve the discomfort. A urinalysis is necessary to determine the proper medication. A special diet, explained below, will help to dissolve crystals in the urine and hasten recovery.

If the cat has an obstruction of the urethra, a catheter is passed into the bladder while he is under a short-acting anesthetic. The catheter is frequently left in place for about 24 hours. The cat is discharged from the hospital when it appears unlikely that obstruction will reoccur, usually 1 - 2 days later. If he is experiencing kidney failure and toxemia, intravenous fluids and additional hospitalization are needed.

How long is treatment continued?

Following initial treatment, you will be asked to return the cat in 7 - 10 days for a recheck of the urine. This is very important because some cats will appear to feel much better, but the urine is still bloody or contains crystals. If medication is stopped based on how the cat appears to feel, treatment may be terminated prematurely and a relapse will probably occur.

Can cystitis occur again?

Many cats have recurrence of cystitis. This is one reason that a virus is suspected as the cause. It is also the reason that a proper diet should be fed in the future.

Are there ways to prevent recurrence?

Two things should be done to help prevent recurrence.

1) The most common type of crystals present in the urine are called struvite. These are dissolvable in acidic urine. Therefore, acidification of your cat's urine can be a significant means of prevention. Several special foods are available for this purpose. However, if your cat's crystals are not struvite, acidification may actually make recurrence more likely. Therefore, if at all possible, the crystals in the urine should be analyzed for their composition. This is the most important step in preventing future problems.

2) Restrict the cat's intake of dry cat food. Though dry foods do not cause cystitis, several studies have shown that the cat's total fluid intake is decreased when dry diets are fed. When the fluid intake is decreased, the urine is more concentrated with minerals and other materials that can cause future episodes of cystitis. Canned foods can result in increased fluid intake and more dilute urine.

However, we know that many cats do not like canned food and that there are several distinct advantages to feeding dry food. Therefore, if there have been only a few infrequent episodes of cystitis, these other factors may be more important.

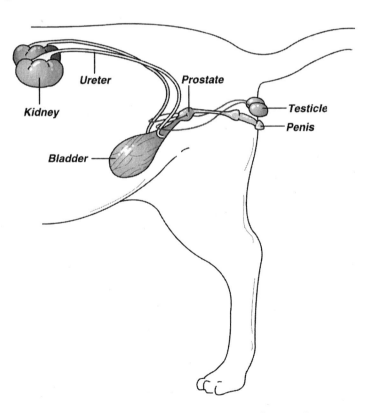

Diagram of urinary and reproductive tract of the male cat.

What complications may occur due to an obstructed urethra?

The most common complication of a urethral obstruction is bladder atony. Atony means that the muscles of the bladder wall are unable to contract to push out urine. This occurs when they are stretched to an extreme degree. Not all cats with obstructions develop atony; in fact, most do not. However, if this occurs, longer hospitalization is necessary. The muscles will nearly always rebound and become functional again, but this may take several days to as long as a week.

Another complication that occurs occasionally is kidney damage. Although feline cystitis does not directly affect the kidneys, but if the bladder becomes extremely enlarged, urine may backup into the kidneys and create enough pressure to temporarily or permanently damage them. If this occurs, prolonged hospitalization will be necessary to treat the kidney damage. However, with aggressive treatment, most cats will recover their normal kidney function.

It should be noted that both complications, bladder atony and kidney damage, are the direct result of the bladder becoming extremely enlarged. Both problems may be prevented by prompt recognition of the problem and prompt medical care.

My male cat has had several urethral obstructions. Can this be prevented?

Male cats that have more than one urethral obstruction can benefit from a surgical procedure called a perineal urethrostomy. The purpose of this is to remove the narrow part of the urethra that is the typical site of the obstruction. Although this prevents future obstructions, some of these cats will still have an occasional recurrence of cystitis, though usually not as severe.

This surgical procedure is also performed if the urethral obstruction is so severe that normal urine flow cannot be reestablished or if there are permanent strictures that develop in the urethra.

Surgically changing the cat's urethra makes him more prone to bacterial infections in the bladder and bladder stones. Therefore, this surgery is only recommended if other means of prevention or treatment are not successful. However, the complications associated with the surgery are not life-threatening like urethral obstructions, so the surgery generally offers a significant benefit for the cat that really needs it.

 DENTAL DISEASE

What kinds of dental problems do cats have?

Dental disease is common in cats, as well as humans. The most common form of dental disease in humans is cavities. This is not the case in cats. The most common form of feline dental disease is tartar buildup. This causes irritation of the gums around the base of the teeth, resulting in exposure of the roots. Ultimately, this leads to infection and tooth loss.

Isn't it correct that cats that eat dry cat food don't have tartar buildup?

There are many misconceptions about tartar buildup in cats. Diet plays more of a minor role than most people think. Because dry food is not as sticky as canned food, it does not adhere to the teeth as much and thus, does not cause tartar buildup as rapidly. However, eating dry food does not remove tartar from the teeth. Once tartar forms, a professional cleaning is necessary. One of the main factors determining the amount of tartar buildup is the individual chemistry in the mouth. Some cats need yearly cleanings; other cats need a cleaning only once every few years.

What does tartar do to the teeth?

If tartar is allowed to remain on the teeth, several things may happen.

1) The tartar will mechanically push the gums away from the roots of the teeth. This allows the teeth to loosen in their sockets and infection to enter the root socket. The teeth will loosen and fall out or have to be extracted.

2) Infection will accumulate in the mouth, resulting in gingivitis (gums), tonsillitis, and pharyngitis (sore throat). Although antibiotics may temporarily suppress the infection, if the tartar is not removed from the teeth, infection will return quickly.

3) Infection within the mouth will be picked up by the blood stream and carried to other parts of the body. Kidney and heart infections frequently begin in the mouth.

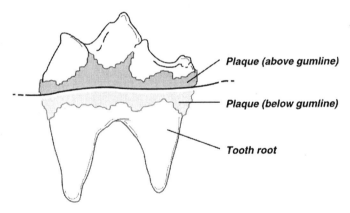

Plaque (above gumline)

Plaque (below gumline)

Tooth root

Molar Tooth with Dental Plaque

What is involved in cleaning my cat's teeth?

Proper cleaning of the teeth requires complete cooperation of the patient so plaque and tartar can be removed properly. Anesthesia is required to thoroughly clean the teeth. Although anesthesia always carries a degree of risk, the modern anesthetics in use in the clinics minimize this risk, even for older cats. Depending on your cat's age and general health status, blood may be analyzed prior to anesthesia to evaluate blood cell counts and organ functions.

There are four steps in the cleaning process that will be used on your cat:

1) **Scaling** removes the tartar above and below the gum line. This is done with hand instruments and ultrasonic cleaning equipment.

2) **Polishing** smooths the surface of the teeth, making them resistant to additional plaque formation.

3) **Flushing** removes dislodged tartar from the teeth and helps to remove the bacteria that accompany tartar.

4) **Fluoride** coating decreases teeth sensitivity, strengthens enamel, and decreases the rate of future plaque formation.

What type of scheduling is needed for teeth cleaning?

You will have to schedule the procedure a few days in advance. It will be necessary to withhold food after 6 PM the night before; please do not remove the water. Your cat should be admitted to the hospital early and will generally be ready for discharge in the late afternoon. The cat will need to stay indoors that evening to insure that no accidents (falls, etc.) occur until complete recovery from anesthesia. If that is not possible, you may elect to have the cat spend the night in the hospital. The cat should be fed and watered lightly that evening and returned to normal feeding the next morning, at which time it should be completely recovered from the anesthetic.

 DIABETES MELLITUS

What is diabetes mellitus?

There are two forms of diabetes in cats: diabetes insipidus and diabetes mellitus. Diabetes insipidus is a very rare disorder that results in failure to regulate body water content. Your cat likely has the more common type of diabetes, diabetes mellitus. This disease is seen on a fairly regular basis, usually in cats 5 years of age or older. Simply put, diabetes mellitus is a failure of the pancreas to regulate blood sugar. The pancreas is a small but vital organ that is located near the stomach. It has two significant populations of cells. One group of cells produces the enzymes necessary for proper digestion. The other group, called beta-cells, produces the hormone called insulin.

Some people with diabetes take insulin shots and others take oral medication. Is this true for cats?

In cats, two types of diabetes mellitus have been discovered. Both types are similar in that there is a failure to regulate blood sugar, but the basic mechanisms of disease differ somewhat between the two groups.

1) **Type I, or Insulin Dependent Diabetes Mellitus**, results from total or near-complete destruction of the beta-cells. This is the most common type of feline diabetes. As the name implies, cats with this type of diabetes require insulin injections to stabilize blood sugar.

2) **Type II, or Non-Insulin Dependent Diabetes Mellitus**, is different because some insulin-producing cells remain. However, the amount produced is insufficient, there is a delayed response in secreting it, and the tissues of the cats body are relatively resistant to it. These cats may be treated with an oral drug that stimulates the remaining functional cells to produce or release insulin in an adequate amount to normalize blood sugar. Alternatively, they may be treated with insulin. Cats with NIDDM may ultimately progress to total beta-cell destruction and then require insulin injections.

Why is insulin so important?

The role of insulin is much like that of a gatekeeper: it stands at the surface of body cells and opens the door, allowing glucose to leave the blood stream and pass inside the cells. Glucose is a vital substance that provides much of the energy needed for life, and it must work *inside* the cells. Without an adequate amount of insulin, glucose is unable to get into the cells. It accumulates in the blood, setting in motion a series of events which can ultimately prove fatal. When insulin is deficient, the cells become starved for a source of energy. In response to this, the body starts breaking down stores of fat and protein to use as alternative energy sources. As a consequence, the cat eats more; thus, we have weight loss in a cat with a ravenous appetite. The body tries to eliminate the excess glucose by eliminating it in the urine. However, glucose (blood sugar) attracts water; thus, urine glucose takes with it large quantities of the body's fluids, resulting in the production of a large amount of urine. To avoid dehydration, the cat drinks more and more water.

Classical signs of diabetes mellitus:

- Weight loss
- Ravenous appetite
- Increased water consumption
- Increased urination

How is diabetes mellitus diagnosed?

The diagnosis of diabetes mellitus is based on three criteria: the four classical clinical signs, the presence of a persistently high level of glucose in the blood stream, and the presence of glucose in the urine. The normal level of glucose in the blood is 80 - 120 mg/dl (3.9 - 6.1 mmol/L). It may rise to 250 - 300 mg/dl 13.8 - 16.5 mmol/L) following a meal or when the cat is very excited. However, diabetes is the only common disease that will cause the blood glucose level to rise above 400 mg/dl (22 mmol/L). Some diabetic cats will have a glucose level as high as 800 mg/dl (44 mmol/L), although most will be in the range of 400 - 600 mg/dl (22 - 33 mmol/L). To keep the body from losing its needed glucose, the kidneys do not allow glucose to be filtered out of the blood stream until an excessive level is reached. This means that cats with a normal blood glucose level will not have glucose in the urine. Diabetic cats, however, have excessive amounts of glucose in the blood, so it will be present in the urine.

What are the implications for me and my cat?

For the diabetic cat, one reality exists: blood glucose cannot be normalized without treatment. Although the cat can go a day or so without treatment and not get into a crisis, treatment should be looked upon as part of the cat's daily routine. Treatment almost always requires some dietary changes. Whether an individual cat will require oral therapy or insulin injections will vary.

There are two implications for the owner: financial commitment and personal commitment. When your cat is well regulated, the maintenance costs are minimal. The special diet, the oral medication, insulin, and syringes are not expensive. However, the financial commitment is significant during the initial regulation process and if complications arise.

Initially, your cat will be hospitalized for a few days to deal with the immediate crisis and to begin the regulation process. The "immediate crisis" is only great if your cat is so sick that it has quit eating and drinking for several days. Cats in this state, called ketoacidosis, may require a week or more of hospitalization with quite a bit of laboratory testing. Otherwise, the initial hospitalization may be only for a day or two to get some testing done and to begin treatment. At that point, your cat goes home for you to administer medication. At first, return visits are required every 3 - 7 days to monitor progress. It may take a month or more to achieve good regulation.

The financial commitment may again be significant if complications arise. Your veterinarian will work with you to try and achieve consistent regulation, but some cats are difficult to keep regulated. It is important that you pay close attention to our instructions related to administration of medication, to diet, and to home monitoring. Another complication that can arise is hypoglycemia or low blood sugar; if severe, it may be fatal. This may occur due to inconsistencies in treatment or because some cats can have a spontaneous remission of their disease. This will be explained in subsequent paragraphs.

Your personal commitment to treating this cat is very important in maintaining regulation and preventing crises. Most diabetic cats require insulin injections twice daily, at about 12 hour intervals. They must be fed the same food in the same amount on the same schedule every day. If you are out of town, your cat must receive proper treatment while you are gone. These factors should be considered carefully before deciding to treat a diabetic cat.

What is involved in treatment?

The best one word answer to that question is consistency. Your cat needs consistent administration of medication, consistent feeding, and a stable, stress-free lifestyle. To best achieve this, it is preferred that your cat live indoors. Although that is not essential, indoor living removes many uncontrollable variables that can disrupt regulation.

The first step in treatment is to alter your cat's diet. Diets that are high in fiber are preferred because they are generally lower in sugar and slower to be digested. This means that the cat does not have to process a large amount of sugar at one time. Prescription Diet Feline r/d™ is fed until the proper weight is achieved, then your cat is switched to one of the others. Your veterinarian can recommend appropriate diets for the diabetic cat.

Your cat's feeding routine is also important. The average cat prefers to eat about 10 - 15 times per day, one mouthful at a time. This means that food is left in the bowl at all times for free choice feeding. However, this is not the best way to feed a diabetic cat. The preferred way is to feed twice daily, just before each insulin injection. If your cat is currently eating on a free choice basis, please try to make the change. However, if your cat will not change or if you have several cats that eat in a free choice fashion, you may find that this change is not practical. If a two-meals-per-day feeding routine will not work for you, it is still very important that you find some way to accurately measure the amount of food that is consumed.

It is estimated that about 25% of diabetic cats have Type II diabetes. This means that they can probably be treated with oral medication instead of insulin injections. There is no reliable, practical test to know if your cat is one of these. Therefore, your cat will be placed on an initial dose of glipizide or glyburide, an oral hypoglycemic drug, for about 1 week. This is usually done at home if your cat is eating well. Weekly blood glucose levels are checked until it is determined whether or not response is occurring. If response occurs and blood sugar declines, this treatment is continued until it is no longer effective. That may be for many years or for only a few months, depending on the progression of destruction of the beta-cells in the pancreas.

The other form of treatment is insulin injections. This approach is used for five classes of cats:

1) Cats that do not take tablets well.

2) Cats belonging to owners who cannot give tablets.

3) Cats that fail to respond to glipizide or glyburide.

4) Cats that have been ketoacidotic (because Type II diabetics rarely become ketoacidotic).

5) Cats belonging to owners who find injections easier to give than tablets.

Many people are initially fearful of giving insulin injections. If this is your initial reaction, consider these points.

1) Insulin does not cause pain when it is injected.

2) The injections are made with very tiny needles that your cat hardly feels.

3) The injections are given just under the skin in areas in which it is almost impossible to cause damage to any vital organ. Your veterinarian will guide you.

Is continual or periodic monitoring needed?

It is necessary that your cat's progress be checked on a regular basis. Monitoring is a joint project on which owners and veterinarians must work together.

Home Monitoring

Your part consists of two forms of monitoring. First, you need to be constantly aware of your cat's appetite, weight, water consumption, and urine output. You should be feeding a constant amount of food each day which will allow you to be aware of days that your cat does not eat all of it or is unusually hungry after the feeding. You should weigh your cat at least once monthly. It is best to use the same scales each time. A baby scale works well for this.

You should develop a way to measure water consumption. The average 10 pound (4.5 kg) cat should drink no more than 7 1/2 oz. (225 ml) of water per 24 hours. Since this is highly variable from one cat to another, keeping a record of your cat's water consumption for a few weeks will allow you to establish what is normal for your cat. Another way to measure water consumption is based on the number of times it drinks each day. When properly regulated, it should drink no more than four times per day. If this is exceeded, you should take steps to make an actual measurement.

Urine output can be measured by determining the amount of litter that is scooped out of the litter box. This is a little less accurate if you have more than one cat that uses the litter box, but it can still be meaningful. The best way to measure litter is to use a clumping litter and scoop it into a sealable container. After a few weeks you will be able to know the normal rate at which the jar fills. Too rapid filling will indicate that your cat's urine production has increased.

Any significant change in your cat's food intake, weight, water intake, or urine output is an indicator that the diabetes is not well controlled. We should see the cat at that time for blood testing.

The second method of home monitoring is to determine the presence of glucose in the urine. If your cat is properly regulated, there should be no glucose present in the urine.

There are several ways to detect glucose in urine. You may purchase urine glucose test strips in any pharmacy. They are designed for use in humans with diabetes, but they will also work in the cat. The use of special non-absorbing kitty litter permits you to dip the test strip into urine in the litter box. Aquarium gravel, Styrofoam packing "peanuts," and commercial non-absorbing litter can be used. Since these are not ideal litter materials, they are best used on a periodic basis.

Another method is as follows:

- Put about 1 tablespoon of wet litter in a small cup. (A clay type litter is required; clumping litter will not work.)

- Add about 1 tablespoon of tap water to the litter and stir.

- Dip a urine glucose test strip into the liquid and read it according to the directions on the bottle.

- The results will be about half of the actual urine glucose amount because of the dilution of the added water.

Another option is CatScan G™. This product consists of small strips of paper that are impregnated with a chemical that reacts to the presence of glucose. They are mixed in normal kitty litter so that at least a few of them are likely to be moistened when your cat urinates. A color change indicates that glucose is present. It is recommended that these be used about twice per week.

If glucose is detected by either method, the test should be repeated the next two days. If it is present each time, you should take your cat for a blood test.

Monitoring of Blood Glucose

Determining the level of glucose in the blood is the most accurate means of monitoring. This should be done about every 3 - 4 months if your cat seems to be well regulated. It should also be done at any time the clinical signs of diabetes are present or if glucose is detected in the urine for two consecutive days.

Timing is important when the blood glucose is determined. Since eating will elevate the blood sugar for several hours, it is best to test the blood at least 6 hours after eating. When testing the blood we want to know the highest and lowest glucose readings for the day. The highest reading should occur just before an injection of insulin is given. The lowest should occur at the time of peak insulin effect. This is usually 5 - 8 hours after an insulin injection, but it should have been determined during the initial regulation process. Therefore, the proper procedure is as follows:

1) Feed your cat its normal morning meal then bring it to the hospital immediately. If you cannot get it to the hospital within 30 minutes, do not feed it. In that situation, bring its food with you.

2) Bring your cat to the hospital early in the morning without giving it insulin.

3) A blood sample will be taken immediately, then your cat is given insulin and fed if it did not eat at home.

4) A second blood sample will be taken at the time of peak insulin effect.

If your cat gets excited or very nervous when riding in the car or being in the hospital, the glucose readings will be falsely elevated. If this occurs, it is best to admit your cat to the hospital the morning (or afternoon) before testing so it can settle down for testing the next day. Otherwise, the tests give limited information.

Does hypoglycemia (low blood sugar) occur in cats?

Hypoglycemia means low blood sugar. If it is below 40 mg/dl (2.2 mmol/L), it can be life-threatening. Hypoglycemia occurs under three conditions:

1) **If the insulin dose is too high.** Although most cats will require the same dose of insulin for long periods of time, it is possible for the cat's insulin requirements to change. However, the most common causes for change are a reduction in food intake and an increase in exercise or activity. The reason for feeding before the insulin injection is so you can know when the appetite changes. *If your cat does not eat, skip that dose of insulin.* If only half of the food is eaten just give a half dose of insulin. *Always remember that it is better for the blood sugar to be too high than too low.*

2) **If too much insulin is given.** This can occur because the insulin was not properly measured in the syringe or because two doses were given. You may forget that you gave it and repeat it, or two people in the family may each give a dose. A chart to record insulin administration will help to prevent the cat being treated twice.

3) **If your cat has a spontaneous remission of the diabetes.** This is a poorly understood phenomenon, but it definitely occurs in many cats. They can be diabetic and on treatment for many months, then suddenly no longer be diabetic. Since this is not predictable and happens quite suddenly, a hypoglycemic crisis ("insulin shock") is usually the first indication.

The most likely time that a cat will become hypoglycemic is the time of peak insulin effect (5 - 8 hours after an insulin injection). When the blood glucose is only mildly low, the cat will be very tired and unresponsive. You may call it and get no response. Within a few hours, the blood glucose will rise, and your cat will return to normal. Since many cats sleep a lot during the day, this important sign is easily missed. Watch for it; it is the first sign of impending problems. If you see it, please bring in your cat for blood testing.

If your cat is slow to recover from this period of lethargy, you should give it corn syrup (1 tablespoon by mouth) or feed one packet of a semi-moist cat food. If there is no response in 15 minutes, repeat the corn syrup or the semi-moist food. If there is still no response, contact your veterinarian immediately for further instructions. (Note: *Diabetic cats should not be fed semi-moist foods except for this situation.*)

If severe hypoglycemia occurs, a cat will have seizures or lose consciousness. This is an emergency that can only be reversed with intravenous administration of glucose. If it occurs during office hours, see your veterinarian immediately. If it occurs at night or on the weekend, call an emergency clinic for instructions.

Tell me more about spontaneous remission.

This is a poorly understood phenomenon that only happens in a few cats. Unfortunately, it can happen rather suddenly so a hypoglycemic crisis may be created when the normal amount of insulin is given. When it occurs, the cat may be normal for a few weeks or for many months. However, diabetes will almost always return. Therefore, you should watch for the typical signs of diabetes then contact us for insulin instructions.

What causes diarrhea?

Diarrhea is not a disease; rather, it is a symptom of many different diseases. Many mild cases of diarrhea can be resolved quickly with simple treatments. Others are the result of fatal illnesses, such as cancer. Even diarrhea caused by mild illnesses may become fatal if treatment is not begun early enough to prevent severe fluid and nutrient losses.

How serious is diarrhea in cats?

We attempt to determine how sick the cat has become as a consequence of the diarrhea. When the cat is systemically ill (i.e., more than one body system is involved), some of the following may be noted:

- Vomiting
- Dehydration
- Loss of appetite
- Abdominal pain
- High fever
- Lethargy
- Bloody and/or watery diarrhea

What types of tests are performed to find the cause?

If diarrhea is associated with several of the above signs, a series of tests is performed in the hope that a diagnosis can be made. This permits more specific treatment. Diagnostic tests may include radiography (x-rays) with or without barium, blood tests, stool cultures, biopsies of the intestinal tract, and exploratory abdominal surgery. Once the diagnosis is known, treatment may include special medications and/or diets, or surgery.

If your cat does not appear systemically ill from diarrhea, the cause may be less serious. Some of the minor causes of diarrhea include stomach or intestinal viruses, intestinal parasites, and dietary indiscretions (such as eating garbage or other offensive or irritating materials).

A minimum number of tests are performed to rule out certain parasites and infections. These cases may be treated with drugs to control the motility of the intestinal tract, drugs that relieve inflammation in the intestinal tract, and, often, a special diet for a few days. This approach allows the body's healing mechanisms to correct the problem. Expect improvement within 2 - 4 days; if this does not occur, a change in medication or further tests are done to better understand the problem.

Please keep your veterinarian informed of lack of expected improvement so that the situation may be managed properly.

DIARRHEA QUESTIONNAIRE

Questions your veterinarian may ask you to help in diagnosis:

- How long has the diarrhea been present?

- Is the diarrhea more severe now than a few days ago?

- Circle the description of each item that applies:

Consistency
> Watery stool
> Stool is the thickness of pancake batter

Blood
> Very bloody stool
> Only sporadic blood present
> Blood not present in stool
> Bright red blood present
> Dark, tarry blood present

Degree/Frequency
> Entire stool is soft or watery
> Only portions of the stool are soft or watery
> Diarrhea with each bowel movement
> Diarrhea is sporadic (some bowel movements are normal)
> Only 1 or 2 bowel movements per day
> More than 4 bowel movements per day

Color
> Stool is dark brown in color
> Stool is very pale in color
> Stool is black and tarry in appearance

Miscellaneous
> Thick mucus or pieces of tissue present in stool
> Loss of bowel control (defecates in the house on the floor)
> Severe straining when having a bowel movement

- Is your cat's appetite normal?

- If not, is it eating at all?

- What have you been feeding your cat during the last week? (Include dog or cat foods, treats, table foods, milk, and anything else that it gets on a daily basis. Also state what percentage of the diet is each item or category.)

- Does your cat have access to foods other than what you feed it? If so, what?

- Has there been a significant diet change in the last few weeks?

- If so, does that correspond with the onset of the diarrhea?

- Is your cat as active as normal?

- Describe any change in water consumption (up or down).

- Has vomiting been occurring? If so, how frequently and for how long?

- Does your cat go outside your house?

- Does your cat go outside your yard?

- Does your cat have access to garbage cans, either within your house or yard or outside your yard?

- Does your cat have toys that it plays with that could have been swallowed?

- Does your cat have access to sewing materials, such as thread or needles, or rubber bands, or string?

- Do you have other dogs or cats that live with this one? If so, does the other pet have diarrhea?

- Do any of the members of your family currently have a diarrhea problem?

- At what phone number may you be reached at if further information is required?

 EAR INFECTIONS (Otitis)

How common are ear infections in cats?

Infections of the external ear canal (outer ear) by bacteria or yeast, are common in dogs, but not very common in cats. We call this otitis externa. The Persian breed appears more prone to ear infections than other breeds of cats.

What are the symptoms of an ear infection?

A cat with an ear infection is uncomfortable and its ear canals are sensitive. The cat shakes its head trying to get the debris and fluid out, and scratches its ears. The ears often become red and inflamed and develop an offensive odor. A black or yellowish discharge commonly occurs.

Don't these symptoms usually suggest ear mites?

Ear mites can cause several of these symptoms, including a black discharge, scratching, and head shaking. However, ear mite infections generally occur most commonly in kittens. Ear mites in adult cats occur most frequently after a kitten carrying mites is introduced into the household. Sometimes, ear mites will create an environment within the ear canal which leads to a secondary infection with bacteria and yeast (fungus). By the time the cat is presented to the veterinarian, the mites may be gone, but a significant ear infection remains.

Since these symptoms are similar and usually mean an infection, can I just go to my veterinarians office and get some medication?

There are several kinds of bacteria and at least one type of fungus which might cause an ear infection. Without knowing the kind of infection present, your veterinarian does not know which drug to use. In some cases, the ear infection may be caused by a foreign body or tumor in the ear canal. Treatment with medication alone will not resolve these problems. Also, the cat must be examined to be sure that the eardrum is intact. Administration of certain medications can result in loss of hearing if the eardrum is ruptured. This determination is made by the veterinarian and must be done in the office.

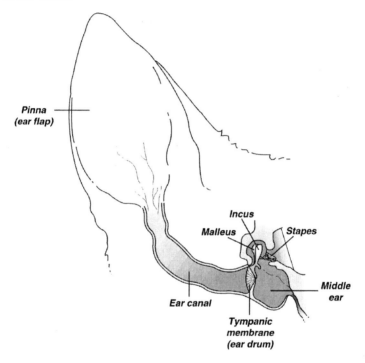

Diagrammatic section of ear showing external ear (pinna and vertical and horizontal canal) and middle ear (ear drum and ossicles: malleus, incus and stapes bones). The inner ear is not shown.

How do you find out which drug to use?

First, the ear canal is examined with an otoscope, an instrument that provides magnification and light. This permits a good view of the ear canal. This examination allows us to determine whether the eardrum is intact and if there is any foreign material in the canal. When the ears are extremely painful and the cat refuses to allow ear examination, sedation with general anaesthesia may be necessary. The next step is to examine a sample of the material from the ear canal to determine which organism is causing the infection. This is called cytology. Examination of that material under the microscope is very important in helping the veterinarian choose the right medication to treat the inflamed ear canal.

How are ear infections treated?

The results of the otoscopic examination and cytology tell your veterinarian what to do. If there is a foreign body or tick lodged in the ear canal, the cat is sedated so that it can be removed. As stated previously, some cats have such a heavy buildup of debris that sedation is needed to cleanse the canal and examine it completely. Cytologic study of debris from the ear canal dictates which drug to use. Sometimes, it reveals the presence of more than one type of infection (i.e., a bacterium and a fungus, or two kinds of bacteria). This situation usually requires the use of multiple medications.

An important part of the evaluation of the patient is the identification of underlying disease. If underlying disease is found, it must be diagnosed and treated, if at all possible. If this cannot be done, the cat is less likely to have a favorable response to treatment. Also, the cat might respond temporarily, but the infection will relapse at a later time (usually when medication is discontinued).

Since ear infections are uncommon in cats, should I be concerned that something else is going on?

Normal cats seem very resistant to ear infections, especially when compared to dogs. Therefore, finding otitis externa in a cat signals us to look for an unusual shape of the ear canal or for something that could affect the cat's immune system. There are two viruses that can cause immune system suppression. Cats with ear infections which cannot be explained should be tested for these two viruses: the feline leukemia virus and the feline immunodeficiency virus (sometimes called the feline AIDS virus). A small amount of blood is needed to test for these viruses. Diabetic cats are also known to have more frequent ear infections than other cats. The diagnosis of diabetes mellitus can be made with blood and urine tests.

What is the prognosis?

In the cat, nearly all ear infections that are properly diagnosed and treated can be cured. However, if an underlying cause remains unidentified and untreated, the outcome will be less favorable. A progress check may be needed before the process is completed, but expect ultimate success. However, the presence of one of the immune suppressing viruses will complicate treatment and will have long term implications on the general health of the cat.

My cat's ear canal is nearly closed. Is that a problem?

Closing of the ear canal occurs when an infection becomes very chronic. There are medications that can shrink the swollen tissues and open the canal in some cats. However, some cases may eventually require surgery.

What is the purpose of the surgery?

The surgery for a closed ear canal is called a lateral ear resection. Its purposes are to remove the vertical part of the ear canal and to remove swollen tissue from the horizontal canal. Removing the vertical canal should be successful, but removal of large amounts of tissue from the horizontal canal is more difficult. In some cases, the ear canal is surgically obliterated. This solves the canal problem, but it leaves the cat deaf on that side.

Is there anything I need to know about getting the medication in the ear?

It is important to get the medication into the horizontal part of the ear canal. This is best done by following theses steps:

- Gently pull the ear flap straight up and hold it with one hand.

- Apply a small amount of medication into the vertical part of the ear canal while continuing to keep the ear flap elevated. Hold this position long enough for the medication to run down to the turn between the vertical and horizontal canal.

- Put one finger in front of and at the base of the ear flap, and put your thumb behind and at the base.

- Massage the ear canal between your finger and thumb. A squishing sound tells you that the medication has gone into the horizontal canal.

- Release the ear and let your cat shake its head. If the medication contains a wax solvent, debris will be dissolved so it can be shaken out.

- If another medication is to be used, apply it in the same manner.

- When all medications have been applied, clean the outer part of the ear canal and the inside of the ear flap with a cotton ball soaked with a small amount of rubbing (isopropyl) alcohol. Do not use cotton tipped applicators to do this as they tend to push debris back into the vertical ear canal.

 ELIMINATION DISORDERS

What is "inappropriate elimination"?

This is a term that means that a cat is urinating and/or defecating in the house but not in the litter box.

What causes it?

There are many possible causes that fall into two general categories:

1) a dislike of the litter box

2) stress-related misbehavior

Why would a cat not like its litter box?

One of the main reasons for this is because the litter box has become objectionable. This usually occurs because it is not cleaned frequently enough or because the cat does not like the material in it. The latter is called substrate aversion; it can occur because the litter was changed to a new, objectionable type or because the cat just got tired of the old litter.

What stresses can cause inappropriate elimination?

There are probably hundreds of these, but the common ones are as follows:

- A new person (especially a baby) in the house

  A person that has recently left the house (permanently or temporarily)
- Several new pieces of furniture
- New drapes
- New carpet
- Rearrangement of the furniture
- Moving to a new house
- A new pet in the house
- A pet that has recently left the house
- A new cat in the neighborhood that can be seen by the indoor cat
- A cat in heat in the neighborhood
- A new dog in the neighborhood that can be heard by the indoor cat

I feel that this is a problem that cannot be tolerated, even if the cat has to leave my house. Is that wrong?

No. Many people are very proud of their home and feel that way.

Can the problem be treated?

Yes, in most cases. However, the treatment is more likely to be successful if several of the following are true:

- The duration is less than 1 month when treatment begins
- There are only one or two locations in the house which the cat uses for inappropriate elimination
- It is possible to identify and relieve the stress-causing situation
- It is possible to neutralize the odor caused by the urine or stool
- You have only one cat

What is involved with treatment?

Most successful treatments rely on a combination of behavior modification techniques and drug therapy.

What are behavior modification techniques, and how are they used?

They can be described as **Aversion Therapy** and **Attraction Therapy**. The former repels the cat from the inappropriate location, and the latter encourages the cat to choose an appropriate location.

The purpose of **Aversion Therapy** is to make the area of inappropriate urination or defecation undesirable for the cat. There are many ways to do this, but the following steps have proven successful in a high percentage of cases.

1) A product to neutralize the odor of urine or stool should be used in places where inappropriate urination or defecation has occurred. If the objectionable location is on carpet, it is necessary to treat the carpet and the pad below because most of the odor will be in the pad. This usually means soaking the carpet with the neutralizing product so it penetrates into the pad. Test an inconspicuous piece of carpet for staining before using any odor neutralizing product.

2) Cover the area(s) with aluminum foil and secure it to the carpet or furniture with masking tape. Aluminum foil is a surface on which most cats will not walk.

3) If the soil in potted plants is being used, place a lemon-scented air freshener at the base of the plant. This will usually repel the cat.

The purpose of **Attraction Therapy** is to make the litter box more desirable than the inappropriate site. The following are usually successful:

1) Purchase a new litter box; even well-cleaned litter boxes have odor deep in the plastic. It is important not to use a litter box with a hood. Although we like our privacy, most cats find a hooded litter box undesirable.

2) Purchase non-scented clumping litter. If your cat has not been using this type of litter, it will usually find it more desirable than the clay types. That increases the chances that the new litter box will be used.

3) Place the new litter box near the area of inappropriate urination until it is used for several days, then move it 2 - 3 feet (0.7 - 1 m) per day back to the desired location.

4) Keep the existing litter box in the normal location in case the aversion therapy causes your cat to return to it.

What drugs are used?

There are several that have been used. Generally, they fall into three categories:

- Anti-depressants, including amitripyline and buspirone
- Tranquilizers, including diazepam and phenobarbital
- Hormones, including megestrol acetate and medroxyprogesterone acetate

Are these drugs approved for use in cats?

No. All of these were developed as anti-depressants or tranquilizers for humans. They should only be used in cats under veterinary supervision and prescription.

I understand that buspirone has gained popularity recently. What is this drug?

Buspirone (trade name Buspar®) is an antidepressant drug prescribed by physicians; it is a human drug, not a veterinary drug. It has been shown to be effective in a significant number of cats with elimination behaviour problems. It should only be used in cats under veterinary prescription and supervision.

What kinds of emergencies might occur?

There are many possible emergencies from road traffic accidents, to acute internal problems such as an intestinal blockage, but the following are the most serious and require immediate attention:

- Any severe difficulty in breathing
- Cardiac failure
- Massive hemorrhage
- Profound shock from any cause
- Anaphylaxis (severe allergic reactions)
- Penetrating wounds of the thorax (chest) or abdomen
- Coma and loss of consciousness
- Poisoning
- Massive injuries to the body

What are some other emergencies where veterinary help must be sought at once?

Seizures, particularly if there is a loss of consciousness. Seizures may be due to epilepsy, head trauma, poisonings or occasionally other medical conditions.

- Burns and scalds
- Heat stroke
- Bites and fight wounds
- Continuous vomiting and/or diarrhea

What can I do while getting veterinary help?

1) Keep calm.
2) Contact the veterinary hospital, appraise them of the situation and get first aid advice.
3) Keep the animal warm, as quiet as possible, and keep movement to a minimum if there is possible trauma - broken limbs, etc.
4) For specific aid refer to the following table.
5) Obtain a suitable container such as a strong cardboard box. Drop a blanket or thick towel over the patient. Tuck in carefully or maneuver animal onto blanket to lift gently into transport container or directly into car.
6) Get to a veterinary hospital as soon as possible, but drive carefully!

Emergency Situation	Action
Road traffic accident	Make sure animal has clear airway (do not put hand in mouth if pet is conscious), keep warm with blanket (also helps restrain if frightened or aggressive). Cover wounds with cleanest material available. Handle with care, supporting body as much as possible. Carry in basket, box or cage to veterinary hospital.
Bleeding (hemorrhage)	If severe hemorrhage from cut or open wound on a limb apply tourniquet above wound just tight enough to significantly reduce flow of blood; has to be loosened within 20 minutes. Apply pad of cotton wool over gauze dressing to wound or bleeding point and bandage firmly and/or apply pressure.
Seizures	Avoid animal injuring itself. Do not put hand in mouth, use handle or similar to prevent teeth clamping tongue. Keep animal as quiet and in the dark as much as possible.
Burns and scalds	Cool the burned area with cool water, for example running water or soaked towels. This also helps remove caustic substances (acid or alkaline) if these are the cause. If loss of skin, cover with cleanest material available.
Heat stroke (animals left in a car in summer with little or no ventilation; excessive panting and obvious distress)	Cool with water.
Hemorrhagic gastroenteritis (diarrhea with blood; with or without vomiting)	Seek veterinary attention.
Bites, fight wounds	Clean with soapy water. Requires veterinary attention and antibiotics.
Poisons	Induce vomiting with 5 mL (teaspoon) of hydrogen peroxide orally or a teaspoon of salt placed in the mouth. Keep sample of vomit. DO NOT INDUCE VOMITING if animal has ingested corrosive material such as strong acid, alkali, or petroleum-based products. If corrosive or toxic material on skin, wash profusely. Bring sample of suspected poison with container to the veterinary hospital.

Eye damage	If cornea penetrated or perforated it will be very painful. Prevent animal scratching at eye and doing further damage. If eyeball out of socket (proptosis) keep moist with saline solution (e.g. contact lens solution) and protect.
Shock (*see below*)	Keep the animal warm and quiet. Seek immediate veterinary help.

What is shock?

Shock has many definitions. It is a complex body reaction to a number of situations. These include acute loss of blood volume such as in hemorrhage, heart failure and other causes of decreased circulation (e.g. severe and sudden allergic reaction and heat stroke). If not treated quickly and effectively shock may cause irreversible injury to body cells, and it can be rapidly fatal.

How do I recognize shock?

Signs include rapid breathing which may be noisy, rapid heart rate with a weak pulse, pale (possibly even white) mucous membranes (for instance gums, lips, under eyelids) and severe depression (listlessness) and cool extremities (limbs and ears). The cat may vomit.

What should I do?

Seek veterinary help immediately. Keep the cat warm and quiet.

 FATTY LIVER SYNDROME

What is the Fatty Liver Syndrome, and how does a cat get it?

The feline Fatty Liver Syndrome (FLS) is also known as feline hepatic lipidosis. This disease is peculiar to cats and is one of the most common liver diseases seen in cats.

The typical cat with the FLS has recently gone through a period of anorexia (not eating). The chances of the FLS occurring are greater if the cat was obese before the anorexia began. As fat is broken down to supply nutrients for the anorectic cat, the fat is deposited so rapidly in the liver that it cannot be processed. It becomes stored in and around the liver cells, resulting in liver failure. The cat often becomes icteric or jaundiced as evidenced by a yellow color in the whites of the eyes or in the skin. At this point, the disease will be fatal if not treated rapidly and aggressively.

How is it diagnosed?

Diagnosis of the FLS is made from blood tests for liver function and from a liver biopsy or aspirate. The latter involves inserting a very tiny needle through the skin and into the liver, removing a small number of liver cells, and examining those cells under the microscope. The FLS cat will have a large amount of fat in and among the liver cells. Generally, other tests are then performed to determine why the cat quit eating. If the cause for anorexia is treatable or resolved, the prognosis is reasonably good.

Is this a treatable disease?

This disease is very treatable, but treatment of the FLS requires that the cat receive nutritional support until the appetite returns. A consistently high quality diet will allow the liver to resume functioning so it may remove the fat. This does not occur quickly; it takes an average of 6 - 7 weeks. Therefore, a method of force feeding such as an esophagostomy tube must be used to allow you to feed your cat at home. Your veterinarian will guide you.

FELINE IMMUNODEFICIENCY VIRUS

Is this the same virus that causes AIDS in people?

No. The Feline Immunodeficiency Virus (FIV) is also called the Feline AIDS Virus. It is likened to the AIDS virus that affects humans because of the similarities in the two diseases which result. Fortunately, most viruses are species specific. This is the case with the human AIDS virus and with FIV. The AIDS virus affects only humans, and the FIV affects only cats.

How do cats get the FIV?

FIV is transmitted primarily by the biting that occurs in cat fights. Other interactions of cats, such as sharing common food and water bowls or grooming each other, have not been shown to be significant in transmission.

How is it diagnosed?

Evidence of exposure to the FIV can be detected by a simple blood test. A positive test means the cat has been exposed to the virus and will likely be infected for the remainder of its life. A negative may mean that the cat has not been exposed; however, false negatives occur in two situations:

- From the time of initial virus inoculation into the cat, it may take up to two years for the test to turn positive. Therefore, for up to two years, the test may be negative even though the virus is present in the cat.

- When some cats become terminally ill with FIV, the test may again turn negative. This occurs because antibodies (immune proteins) produced against the virus become attached and bound to the large amount of virus present. Since the test detects antibodies which are free in circulation, the test may be falsely negative. This is not the normal occurrence, but it does happen to some cats.

What does a positive test result mean in a kitten?

The vast majority of kittens under 4 months of age who test positive have not been exposed to the virus. Instead, the test is detecting the immunity (antibodies) that were passed from the mother to the kitten. These antibodies may persist until the kitten is about 6 months old. Therefore, the kitten should be retested at about 6 months of age. If it remains positive, the possibility of true infection is much greater. If the kitten tests negative, there is nothing to worry about.

How can a kitten become infected?

If a kitten is bitten by an FIV infected cat, it can develop a true infection. However, the test will usually not turn positive for many months. If a mother cat is infected with the FIV at the time she is pregnant or nursing, she can pass large quantities of the virus to her kittens. This means of transmission may result in a positive test result in just a few weeks.

What type of disease does the FIV cause?

An FIV infected cat will generally go through a prolonged period of viral dormancy before it becomes ill. This incubation period may last as long as 6 years. Thus, your veterinarian generally does not diagnosis an FIV sick cat at an early age.

When illness occurs, a variety of severe chronic illnesses is seen. The most common illness is a severe infection affecting the gums. Abscesses from fight wounds that should heal within a week or two may remain active for several months. Respiratory infections may linger for weeks. The cat may lose weight and go through periods of not eating well; the hair coat may become unkempt. The cat may have episodes of treatment-resistant diarrhea. Ultimately, widespread organ failure occurs, and the cat dies.

Is there a treatment for it?

There is no treatment that will rid the cat of the FIV. Sometimes, the disease state can be treated and the cat experiences a period of recovery and relatively good health. However, the virus will still be in the cat and may become active at a later date. Therefore, the long term prognosis is not good.

What should I do with a cat that is FIV positive but is not ill?

If you have a cat that tests FIV positive but is not ill, it is not necessary to euthanize it immediately. As long as it does not fight with your other cats or those of your neighbors, transmission is not likely to occur. However, if it is prone to fight or if another cat often instigates fights with it, transmission is likely. In fairness to your neighbors, it is generally recommended to restrict a FIV-positive cat to your house. Owners of infected cats must be responsible so that the likelihood of transmission to someone else's cat is minimized.

Is there a vaccine for FIV?

Unfortunately, there is no vaccine available against FIV.

What is Feline Infectious Anemia and what does it do to the cat?

Feline Infectious Anemia (FIA) is a blood disease of cats caused by *Hemobartonella felis* (*H. felis*). *H. felis* attaches to the cat's red blood cells. When the immune system detects this abnormality, it destroys the blood cells. This results in the cat having a shortage of red blood cells, which is the same as being anemic.

How does a cat get FIA?

We are not sure of the means of transmission of FIA. There is speculation that it can be passed from one cat to another by insects that can carry blood; fleas, ticks, and mosquitoes have been considered potential vectors (carriers) of the parasite between cats. However, none of these have been proven.

How is FIA diagnosed?

The presence of *H. felis* on a few red blood cells does not mean that the cat has Feline Infectious Anemia. In fact, *H. felis* is commonly found on the red blood cells of normal cats. In almost all cases of FIA, the cat has encountered another disease or another form of stress. This state of debilitation then triggers *H. felis* and allows the development of FIA. Diagnosis of this disease is made from a blood sample. If the cat is anemic and large numbers of *H. felis* are present, the diagnosis of FIA is made. Unfortunately, *H. felis* is not always present on the cat's red blood cells because it appears in the blood stream in cycles. If FIA is suspected, it may be necessary to examine several blood samples before *H. felis* is identified.

Is it true that this disease is associated with the leukemia virus?

Since about 20% of cats with FIA are infected with the Feline Leukemia Virus (FeLV), a blood test should be performed to detect this virus. This virus can serve as the stress factor that allows the development of FIA. If the FeLV is found, the short-term prognosis is usually good, but the long-term prognosis will be poor because of the diseases which are caused by the feline leukemia virus.

Is FIA treatable?

Treatment is relatively simple and generally successful. Oral medications that suppress *H. felis* are used for several weeks. If the cat is severely anemic, a blood transfusion may be needed.

Since the drugs only suppress *H. felis* and do not completely rid the cat of it, FIA may occur again. Keeping your cat properly vaccinated, feeding it a high quality food, and treating other illnesses promptly will reduce the chances of another episode of FIA.

What causes Feline Infectious Peritonitis?

Feline Infectious Peritonitis (FIP) is a severe disease of domestic cats and some exotic cats. It does not affect non-feline species, such as dogs. It is caused by a coronavirus. The incubation period is controversial. In experiments with the virus, cats will develop the disease within 2 weeks of infection. However, in household situations, it appears that the virus may be dormant in some cats for several months, or even years, before the disease occurs.

What are the clinical signs?

FIP is a chronic, wasting disease that results in poor appetite, fever, and weight loss over several weeks; it is ultimately fatal. Because various organs may be affected (i.e., liver, kidneys, brain, eyes, etc.), a variety of clinical signs may be associated with this disease. For example, blindness or seizures may occur in one cat, while another will have signs of liver disease (jaundice). There are two forms, the **wet (effusive) form** and the **dry form**. The **wet form** results in accumulation of large quantities of fluid in the chest or abdomen. If it occurs in the chest, the cat will experience difficulty breathing. When it occurs in the abdomen, a large, bloated appearance will result. The **dry form** affects the target organs in a similar fashion, but no fluid is produced. If enough time passes without the cat dying, the dry form may progress into the wet form. Diagnosis of FIP is much easier if fluid is present.

How is FIP diagnosed?

Diagnosis of FIP may be difficult and frustrating. There are no specific tests which are reliable in all cases. Although organ biopsy is the most reliable, this requires surgery. For obvious reasons, surgery may not be advisable in a sick cat. The following tests may be used on cats with suspicious clinical signs.

1) **Coronavirus Test.** This test detects antibodies to any coronavirus. Antibodies are the circulating defense agents of the immune system. There are two coronaviruses that affect the cat: the FIP virus and the enteric coronavirus. If positive, this test indicates that one or both of those viruses WAS or IS present in the cat. However, it is not known which virus is reacting to the test. Since antibodies may persist even if the virus is no longer present, a positive test can be misleading in some cases. Also, terminally ill cats may have their antibodies "tied up" when large amounts of the FIP virus are present. This can result in a false negative test result. Therefore, this test must be interpreted in conjunction with results of other tests. These tests are listed below.

2) **Polymerase Chain Reaction (PCR) Test.** This new test is more specific for the FIP virus than the coronavirus antibody test; however, it is still just a test for the presence of the FIP virus. A positive test means the virus is present, but does not necessarily mean the disease is present. This test is also subject to some false negative results.

3) **Serum Protein Levels.** If the total serum protein is elevated AND the A:G ratio (ratio of two different blood proteins) is less than normal, FIP becomes a more likely diagnosis. A few other diseases may also cause this, but these are also very severe and usually fatal. These findings occur in 50% of the cases of FIP.

4) **White Blood Cell Count.** If the white blood cell count is greater than 25,000 cells/μl, FIP becomes a stronger possibility. However, several other diseases may cause this and some of these are not fatal. Also, many cases of FIP have a normal white blood cell count (less than 18,000 cells/μl).

5) **Abdominal/Chest Fluid Analysis.** If fluid is present, this is a very meaningful test. If the characteristics of the fluid are appropriate and the cat has the correct clinical signs, a diagnosis can be made with greater assurance. Unfortunately, this fluid is not present in the dry form of FIP.

6) **Fine Needle Aspiration of the Liver or Kidneys.** A few cells may be aspirated from the liver or kidney without stressing the cat (i.e., with a local anesthetic in the skin). FIP produces a particular inflammatory pattern in these organs which, although not diagnostic, is strongly suggestive for the disease. This helps to rule out other diseases.

7) **Radiographs (X-rays) of Chest or Abdomen.** Radiographs serve to identify enlargements in organs and the presence of fluid in the chest or abdomen. They are helpful but not diagnostic and are used to decide which other tests are appropriate.

8) **A combination of three blood tests.** Cats with the combination of a low lymphocyte (a white blood cell) count, a high blood globulin (protein) level, and a positive coronavirus antibody test have been shown to have a 94% chance of having FIP.

9) **Organ biopsy.** Organ biopsy is the only test which is diagnostic of FIP. However, it is not always possible since the organ involved may be the eye or the brain.

A case workup in the absence of organ biopsy often includes several or all of the above tests. Strongly suggestive findings with several tests often provides the basis for a presumptive diagnosis of FIP.

Is FIP contagious?

As with other viruses, spread of infection to other cats is a concern. However, there are three stages of FIP infection, and significant risk to other cats occurs in only the first two stages.

1) The first stage is initial infection. During the two to four week period following viral infection of the cat, a large amount of virus is shed; other cats in direct contact with virus will be exposed.

2) The second stage is one of dormancy. The virus is inactive within the cat, so it causes no disease. If the cat is stressed during this stage, some virus shedding may occur. Otherwise, the cat is not contagious. This stage may last a few weeks to several years.

3) The third stage is clinical illness. It usually lasts a few weeks and terminates in death of the cat. As a rule, the cat is not contagious during this stage.

What is the treatment and prognosis for a cat with FIP?

Many treatments have been tried for cats with FIP, but none have been consistently successful. Apparently, an occasional cat will recover, but this is the exception rather than the rule. Removing fluid from the chest or abdomen in cats with the wet form will make them comfortable for a short while, and a few drugs will make some of them feel better. However, there is no known curative treatment. The prognosis for a cat with FIP is very poor. Once a reasonably reliable presumptive diagnosis has been made, euthanasia is often the most appropriate course of action.

Is there a way to disinfect the premises?

The coronavirus may live for up to 3 weeks in the environment. If viral shedding into the environment seems likely, a 1:30 mixture of household bleach and water (i.e., 1 cup of bleach in a gallon of water) should be used to disinfect food and water bowls, litter pans, cages, bedding material, and items that will not be adversely affected by household bleach.

What about prevention?

A preventive vaccine against FIP is available, but neither veterinarians nor the manufacturer recommend that the vaccine be given routinely to all cats. The vaccine is generally recommended for cats in contact with free-roaming cats or for those living in households that have had a cat with FIP. Initially, two doses are given at a 2 - 4 week interval. An annual booster is needed to maintain immunity.

FELINE LEUKEMIA VIRUS DISEASES

F eline leukemia virus infection was, until recently, the most common fatal disease of cats. Because we can now protect cats with a leukemia virus vaccine, we are seeing fewer cases of the disease. However, it still remains a major cause of death in cats.

"Leukemia" means cancer of the white blood cells. This was the first disease associated with the feline leukemia virus (FeLV) and, thus, the source of its name. We often use the term "leukemia" rather loosely to include all of the diseases associated with the virus, even though most are not cancers of the blood. This virus causes many other fatal diseases, in addition to leukemia.

What diseases are caused by the FeLV?

There are three major disease categories associated with the FeLV:

1) The Leukemias are cancers of the white blood cells.

2) Lymphosarcoma is a cancer of many different organs but it begins in lymphoid tissue, such as a lymph node. Almost any tissue may be affected; organs commonly involved include lymph nodes, intestinal tract, kidneys, liver, spinal cord, brain, bone marrow and blood.

3) The Non-Cancerous Diseases include a variety of somewhat unrelated diseases. Anemia, abortion, arthritis, and immune suppression are examples. When the immune system is suppressed, the cat becomes susceptible to many diseases it would ordinarily resist and mild diseases, such as respiratory infections, may become fatal.

How is the virus transmitted?

The main means of transmitting the virus is through cat fights. Because large quantities of the FeLV are shed in cat saliva, puncture wounds associated with fighting result in injection of the virus into other cats. Other less frequent routes of viral spread include sharing food and water bowls, cats grooming each other, and transmission from mother to kittens before birth.

What is a "leukemia test"?

The "leukemia test" is used to determine if a cat harbors the virus. Any of three different tests may be used to detect one particular virus protein in the cat. Some tests detect earlier stages of infection, whereas others are used to detect later (i.e., irreversible) stages of infection.

1) The blood ELISA test is performed on a blood sample and detects the FeLV at any stage of infection. This test turns positive within a few days of infection and, in some cases, may later turn negative if the cat's immune system eliminates the infection.

2) The IFA test is performed on a blood smear and turns positive only after the FeLV infection has progressed to a late stage of infection. Once positive, the IFA test usually means that the cat has a permanent infection. A cat who tests IFA positive is only rarely able to successfully eliminate the virus.

3) The tears/saliva ELISA test is performed on a sample of tears or saliva. It turns positive only in a late stage of infection; therefore, it may yield a false negative result in cats who are in the early stage of FeLV infection. It also has been associated with some false positive results due to inherent errors in the way the test is performed. Because of these problems, the tears and saliva tests are not used routinely.

What can happen if a cat is infected with the FeLV?

When we are exposed to a virus, such as a flu virus, there are two possible outcomes. Either our immune system responds to the challenge and protects us, or it is unable to respond successfully, and we develop the flu. A number of factors determine which outcome occurs and whether or not we will get sick:

1) The amount of the virus — did someone sneeze directly in your face?

2) The strain of the virus — some strains are more potent than others.

3) The status of our immune system — are immune suppressing drugs being taken?

4) Age — the very young and very old are more likely to become infected.

5) The presence of other infections which might cause debilitation.

The behavior of the feline leukemia virus in the cat's body is not so black or white. Instead of the two possible outcomes described above (i.e., we get sick or we get well), there are four possible outcomes for cats with FeLV. Understanding these allows one to more fully comprehend some of the unusual situations which may arise in cats.

OUTCOME 1: IMMUNITY

The cat mounts an immune response, eliminating the infection.

This is the most desired outcome because it means that the cat will not become persistently infected with the virus. During this period of virus challenge, the cat may actually develop a mild form of illness. Fever, poor appetite, lethargy, and swollen glands (lymph nodes) in the neck may develop and last for 3 to 10 days. Outcome 1 occurs about 40% of the time after a cat is challenged by the FeLV. Immunity to the virus is more likely to develop in the adult cat than in the kitten.

OUTCOME 2: INFECTION

The cat's immune system is overwhelmed by the virus.

This is the least desired outcome because the cat is persistently infected with FeLV. All three of the FeLV tests will become positive and remain positive for the rest of the cat's life. Although the cat may be sick for a few days initially (as described above), it usually recovers and appears normal for weeks, months, or years. Ultimately, most of these cats die of FeLV-related disease, but as many as 50% will still be healthy after 2 - 3 years and 15% after 4 years. Vaccination of these cats will not cause any problems but doesn't help the cat, either.

Outcome 2 occurs about 30% of the time after a cat is challenged by FeLV. Although infection is more likely to occur in the kitten, many cats are persistently infected as adults. Although the main mode of viral transmission is through bite wounds (saliva), direct daily contact with a FeLV infected cat will often result in transmission of the virus. Non-infected exposed cats are at risk and should be vaccinated, although daily viral contact will result in vaccination failure of some cats.

OUTCOME 3: LATENCY

The cat harbors the virus, but it is not easily detected.

Unlike other viruses, the FeLV does not directly kill the cat's cells or make them become cancerous. Instead, it inserts a copy of its own genetic material (called DNA) into the cat's cells; these cells may later be transformed into cancer cells or cells which will no longer function normally. In Outcome 3, the genetic change in the cat's cells will remain undetected for an average of 2 1/2 years, during which time the cat will appear completely normal.

In the early stages of infection, the blood ELISA test will be positive, but it will turn negative about 2 - 4 weeks later. Following that, the blood ELISA and the IFA tests will remain consistently negative. The PCR test, a recently available diagnostic tool, will detect the latent infection. However, this test is somewhat expensive and not widely available so it is not used for routine testing.

The prospect of latent infection presents a frustrating situation. Latency is estimated to occur about 30% of the time; it leaves the cat in a precarious situation. Some cats will ultimately reject the abnormal cells, and the state of latency will be terminated. In other cats these abnormal cells will result in the production of new FeLV which will result in Outcome 2. Outcome 2 generally leads to death due to a FeLV disease.

Latency is the state that explains the following situations:

1) Latently infected cats will test negative on any FeLV test. If they are vaccinated, they will not be protected. They may develop a fatal FeLV-related disease later, especially following some form of stress or the administration of steroids. Stressors that may activate latent infections include pregnancy and nursing, overcrowding, movement to a new environment, territorial conflicts, poor nutrition, and other diseases. Steroids are used commonly in cats because they are very beneficial for many feline diseases.

2) Lymphosarcoma is the form of cancer normally caused by the FeLV. Cats that have some form of lymphosarcoma normally test positive with any FeLV test. Latently infected cats may have lymphosarcoma and test negative on the FeLV tests. It is also thought that some cats successfully eliminate the virus but not before malignant transformation of cells has already occurred. This may be another explanation for FeLV-negative cats with lymphosarcoma.

3) Latently infected pregnant cats may test FeLV negative (and even be vaccinated) but pass the FeLV to their kittens through nursing. These kittens often experience Outcome 2.

OUTCOME 4: IMMUNE CARRIER

The cat becomes an immune carrier. The FeLV becomes hidden in some of the cat's epithelial cells. Although the FeLV is multiplying, it is not able to get out of these cells because the cat is producing antibodies against the virus. The cat will appear normal in every way, except for its test results. The immune carrier will have a positive blood ELISA test and a negative IFA test.

This situation is unlikely to happen; it is estimated to occur 1 - 2% of the time. These cats may revert to an active FeLV infection (Outcome 2) or may develop a latent infection (Outcome 3). The main reason for understanding this situation is that it explains conflicting FeLV test results. Otherwise, there is not a specific test to detect it.

How are cats with leukemia treated?

Some forms of leukemia (blood cancer) are unresponsive to all available forms of cancer treatment. Other types of leukemias may respond to chemotherapy, though most of these have an average survival time of less than one year. Because the virus is not affected by treatment, the cat will always remain infected with FeLV. Also, relapse of leukemia is possible (and expected). These factors will cause your veterinarian to recommend treatment of leukemia in only a few situations.

What should I do to disinfect my house?

The FeLV lives, at most, only a few hours outside the cat if the environment is dry. Therefore, extensive environmental disinfection is not necessary. If you wait even 2 days to get a new cat, you can be assured that none of the virus from a previous cat will remain in your house.

I have a healthy cat that is infected with the virus. What does that mean?

Healthy infected cats may remain apparently unaffected by the virus for several years. However, such cats should be considered infectious and potentially dangerous to other cats. Such cats should be isolated from non-infected cats to prevent spread of infection. Many people find this undesirable or impossible and elect euthanasia to protect non-infected cats.

Is there any danger to my family?

Extensive tests have been conducted for over 15 years to determine if the FeLV can be transmitted to humans. Thus far, no conclusive evidence has shown any FeLV-related disease in humans or other animal species, including the dog. However, persons with compromised immune systems are of concern to many researchers. Newborn babies, persons on chemotherapy, AIDS patients or transplant recipients on anti-rejection drugs should probably not be unnecessarily exposed to this or any other virus.

Can I protect my other cats?

A vaccine is available to protect cats from the FeLV. Although not 100% of cats are totally protected, the vaccine is strongly recommended for cats who are exposed to open populations of cats, (i.e., outdoor cats). We have seen a definite decline in the incidence of feline leukemia virus infection and related diseases since vaccine use became widespread. It is strongly recommended. If your cat stays indoors at all times and is not in contact with another cat that goes outdoors, the need for the vaccine is minimal.

Cats who are already infected with the FeLV will not be helped by the vaccine. (They will not be hurt by it, either). Pre-vaccination testing for the FeLV is recommended for:

1) cats with a history of cat fights or fight wounds (i.e., abscesses)

2) cats exposed to FeLV-infected cats

3) cats from unknown backgrounds (particularly animal shelters, humane societies, or pet shops)

4) routine health care, especially in multicat households

Will vaccinating my cat with the FeLV vaccine cause the leukemia test to be positive?

No. The vaccine will not cause a cat to test positive for the virus. While the history of vaccination is important to know, it does not alter the ability to interpret the feline leukemia virus test.

Why do cats fight?

Cats are very territorial. They fight with other cats to protect their territory or to acquire more territory. As a result, fight wounds are common in cats. These wounds frequently result in an infection that can be quite debilitating, especially if left untreated. Fight wounds are more common in male cats than in females.

I had my male cat neutered. Why is he still fighting?

The difference between neutered and intact male cats is the desire for more territory. Not only do intact tom cats claim an area around their home, but they continually try to expand the borders of their territory. Because of the desire for more territory and because they do not want intruders in their territory, they are constantly fighting with other cats. In contrast, neutered cats seem content to claim a small area around or within their home. If their territory is breached by another cat, however, they will defend it by fighting. Female cats, whether intact or spayed, will also defend their territory.

How do cat and dog fight wounds differ?

When a dog bites a cat or another dog, it bites into the skin, clamps its teeth shut, and shakes its head. Usually the skin of the victim tears, leaving a large laceration. However, when a cat bites, its teeth go through the skin, and then it releases quickly. This results in small puncture wounds in the skin, with holes about the same diameter as the cat's teeth. These holes seal within hours, trapping bacteria from the cat's mouth under the skin of the victim. Within 24 hours, the holes in the skin are almost impossible to find.

How does this result in an abscess?

The bacteria which are trapped under the skin can multiply for several days before any signs of infection become evident. Swelling and pain at the puncture site are the most common signs of infection; many times, the cat will also run a fever. If loose skin is present around the puncture sites, a pocket of pus will form an abscess. If the skin is not loose, such as on a foot or the tail, the infection spreads throughout the tissues and causes swelling and pain; this type of infection is called cellulitis.

How are fight wound infections treated?

Treatment of cat bite wounds varies. If you know that your cat has bite wounds from a fight, antibiotics given within 24 hours will usually stop spread of the infection and development of an abscess. If several days have elapsed since the fight, an abscess will usually form. The abscess must be drained through the bite wound holes or by incising the skin over the abscess. Occasionally, a latex drain tube must be placed to keep the wound open and allow pus to drain out completely.

Antibiotics given by injection and/or by mouth complete the treatment. The abscess usually heals within 2 - 5 days. If cellulitis occurs instead of an abscess, drainage is not possible because the infection is not confined to a local area. In this case, antibiotics are the sole treatment. Cellulitis is slower to heal than an abscess but will usually take place within 3 - 7 days.

Are there any other possible problems associated with fight wound infections?

Bite wounds are one of the main routes of transmitting the feline leukemia virus between cats. Because this virus is found in large amounts in the saliva of infected cats, bite wounds from these cats are literally injections of virus. When a cat has a fight wound infection and has not been vaccinated against feline leukemia virus, it is usually recommended to test the cat for the presence of the virus. It will take at least 2 - 3 weeks before the leukemia virus infection is advanced enough to be detected. The test should be performed at that time. If the test is negative, you should vaccinate your cat against the virus.

The feline immunodeficiency virus, also called the feline AIDS virus, is also transmitted by bite wounds. Because of an extended incubation period, the test for this virus may not become positive for many months, or even years. Therefore, testing in 2 - 3 weeks is not likely to be meaningful. However, if your cat has been in other fights, testing for this virus could detect an infection that began months earlier.

If a bite wound infection does not heal within a few days, it often becomes necessary to look for an underlying cause. Certain viruses, including the feline leukemia virus and the feline immunodeficiency virus, suppress the immune system and complicate the cat's recovery from infections. A blood test should be performed for the leukemia virus and the feline immunodeficiency virus; if these are negative, other tests may be needed to look for possible explanations.

 FLEAS

What should I do to kill the fleas on my cat?

This is a simple question with a rather complex answer. Successful flea control has two aspects. Fleas must be controlled on your cat, and fleas must be controlled in your cat's environment. Since cats and dogs share the same fleas, the presence of a dog in your cat's environment makes flea control much more difficult. To appreciate the complex issue of flea control, you must understand something about the flea's life cycle.

Fleas seem to be rather simple creatures. How complicated can their life cycle be?

Although you are only able to see the adult flea, there are actually 4 stages of the life cycle. The adult flea constitutes only about 5% of the entire flea population if you consider all four stages of the life cycle. Flea eggs are pearly white and about 1/32" (1/2 mm) in length. They are too small to see without magnification. Fleas lay their eggs on the cat, but the eggs do not stick to the cat's hair. Instead, they fall off into the cat's environment. The eggs make up 50% of the flea population. They hatch into larvae in 1 to 10 days, depending on temperature and humidity. High humidity and temperature favor rapid hatching.

Flea larvae are slender and about 1/8 - 1/4" (2 to 5 mm) in length. They feed on organic debris found in their environment and on adult flea feces, which are essential for successful development. They avoid direct sunlight and actively move deep into carpet fibers or under organic debris (grass, branches, leaves, or soil). They live for 5 to 11 days before becoming a pupa.

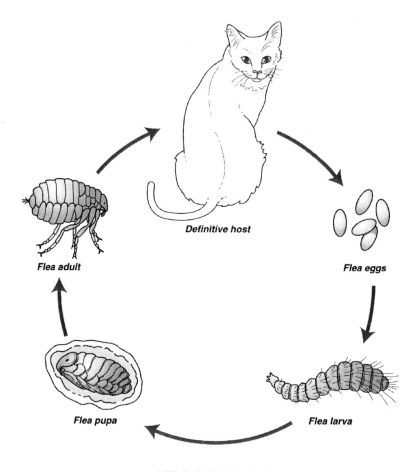

Definitive host

Flea adult

Flea eggs

Flea pupa

Flea larva

LIFE CYCLE OF CAT FLEA

Moisture is essential for their survival; flea larvae are killed by drying. Therefore, it is unlikely that they survive outdoors in shade-free areas. Outdoor larval development occurs only where the ground is shaded and moist and where flea-infested pets spend a significant amount of time. This allows flea feces to be deposited in the environment. In an indoor environment, larvae survive best in the protected environment of carpet or in cracks between hardwood floors. They also thrive in humid climates.

Following complete development, the mature larvae produce a silk-like cocoon in which the next step of development, the pupa, resides. The cocoon is sticky, so it quickly becomes coated with debris from the environment. This serves to camouflage it. In warm, humid conditions, pupae become adult fleas in 5 - 10 days. However, the adults do not emerge from the cocoon unless stimulated by physical pressure, carbon dioxide, or heat.

Pre-emerged adult fleas can survive up to 140 days within the cocoon. During this time, they are resistant to insecticides applied to their environment. Because of this, adult fleas may continue to emerge into the environment for up to 3 weeks following insecticide application.

When the adult flea emerges from its cocoon, it immediately seeks a host because it must have a blood meal within a few days to survive. It is attracted to people and pets by body heat, movement, and exhaled carbon dioxide. It seeks light, which means that it migrates to the surface of the carpet so that it can encounter a passing host. Following the first blood meal, female fleas begin egg production within 36 to 48 hours. Egg production can continue for as long as 100 days, which means that a single flea can produce thousands of eggs.

This entire life cycle (adult flea —> egg —> larvae —> pupa —> adult) can be completed in 14 - 21 days with the proper temperature and humidity conditions. This adds to the problem of flea control.

What can these fleas do to my cat?

If untreated, the female flea will continue to take blood for several weeks. During that time, she will consume about 15 times her body weight in blood. Although the male fleas do not take as much blood, they, too, contribute to significant blood loss. This can lead to the cat having an insufficient number of red blood cells, which is known as anemia. In young or debilitated cats, the anemia may be severe enough to cause death.

Contrary to popular belief, most cats have rather limited itching due to flea bites. However, many cats become allergic to the saliva in the flea's mouth. When these cats are bitten, intense itching occurs, causing the cat to scratch and chew on its skin.

What can I do to rid my cat of fleas?

Successful flea control must rid the cat of fleas and it must rid the cat's environment of fleas. In fact, environmental control is probably more important than what is done to the cat.

If your cat remains indoors and you do not have other pets that come in from the outside, environmental control is relatively easy. However, the cat that goes outdoors or stays outdoors presents a significant challenge. It may be impossible to completely rid the environment of fleas under these conditions, though flea control should still be attempted.

What can I do to my cat?

Many insecticides that are applied to the cat have limited effectiveness against fleas because they are only effective for a few hours after application. Also, these are primarily to kill adult fleas. Flea powders, sprays, and shampoos will kill the fleas present on your cat at the time of application. However, most of these products have little or no residual effects, so the fleas that return to your cat from the environment are not affected. Thus, your cat may be covered with fleas within a day after having a flea bath or being sprayed or powdered. However, there are some newer, more effective sprays that can be a valuable part of the overall treatment plan. They kill adult fleas rapidly and are safe enough to use daily, if necessary. Flea sprays containing insect growth regulators are helpful in managing the overall problem because they help to break the flea life cycle. Some of the newer sprays with growth regulators are not recommended for daily use; once weekly application is recommended. Always read the label when using any new product on a cat.

There are currently some other types of products available that have residual effects (i.e., that last for days to weeks). These include flea collars, flea dips, and the newer monthly products. Flea dip is poured over your cat after it has been bathed. The dip is not rinsed off; rather, it is allowed to dry on the skin and hair. This results in residual flea control for 4 - 5 days. Flea collars are on the cat and working 24 hours per day. The newer monthly products are available as a tablet that prohibits female fleas from laying viable eggs, and as topical products that kill adult fleas. The monthly products are effective and safe and are the recommended approach.

What can I do to my cat's environment?

Environmental flea control usually must be directed at your house and your yard. Even though fleas may be in your house, most people never see them. Fleas greatly prefer cats and dogs to people; they only infest humans when there has not been a cat or dog in the house for several days. (There are exceptions to this.) A professional exterminator may be called to treat your house or you may use a house fogger or a long-lasting spray. These foggers and sprays are very effective for adult fleas, but they will not kill adults that are still in their cocoon. You should purchase a fogger or a spray that kills the adult fleas and inhibits development of the eggs and larvae. In climates with extended warm temperatures and high humidity, it may be necessary to treat two or three times with a 30-day residual product before all stages of the fleas are removed from the house. The second treatment is most effective if it is done 2 weeks after the first.

Yard control may also be done by a professional exterminator or with various insecticides you may use yourself. Be sure that any insecticide that you use has a 30-day residual. This keeps you from having to spray every week. In climates with extended warm temperatures and high humidity, it will often be necessary to treat monthly during the warm months of the year. You should use a 30-day residual product each time. Some of the newest products which contain the growth regulator fenoxycarb are labeled for use only once or twice a year. Your veterinarian is able to help you choose the most effective product for your situation.

I have heard of a treatment for the house that is guaranteed for 1 year. Is that for real?

There is at least one company that will treat your carpet with a flea-killing powder. The powder is non-toxic to people. It is worked deeply into the carpet to prevent it from being removed by vacuuming. This treatment has proven very successful, even in the face of heavy flea infestations. However, the treatment does not address fleas in your yard. The same chemical, a form of boric acid, is also available for application by the home owner. However, the self application kits do not offer the year guarantee. Another option is a treatment which contains the insect growth regulator, fenoxycarb. As stated previously, these products are recommended for use once or twice a year. Fenoxycarb has no activity against adult fleas but is very helpful in inhibiting the development of eggs and larvae. It is a hormone-like substance which works against the juvenile stages of the flea; it is not an insecticide and is therefore a safe choice when children are in the home.

I have not seen fleas on my cat. Does that mean that none are present?

When a cat is heavily infested with fleas, it is easy to find them. If the numbers are small, it is best to quickly turn your cat over and look on its belly. If you do not find them there, look on the back just in front of the tail. Be sure to part the hair and look at the level of the skin. When the numbers are very small, look for "flea dirt." Flea dirt is fecal matter from the flea that contains digested blood. Finding flea dirt is a sure indication that fleas are present or have been present recently.

Flea dirt looks like pepper. It varies from tiny black dots to tubular structures about 1/32" (1/2 mm) long. If you are in doubt of its identification, put the suspected material on a light colored table top or counter top. Add one or two drops of water, and wait about 30 seconds. If it is flea dirt, the water will turn reddish brown as the blood residue goes into solution. Another method is to put some of the material on a white paper towel and then wet the paper towel with water. A red stain will become apparent if you gently wipe the material across the surface of the paper towel. Many people find tiny drops of blood in a cat's bedding or where the cat sleeps. This is usually flea dirt that was moistened, then dried. It leaves a reddish stain on the bedding material and is another sign that fleas are present.

I just got my cat home from boarding and it has fleas. Doesn't that mean that it got them at the boarding facility?

Not necessarily. If you recall, pre-emerged adult fleas can survive up to 140 days within the cocoon. This is significant when your pets are gone from home for extended periods of time. During the time that the house is quiet and empty, pre-emerged adults remain in their cocoon. Even if the house was treated with an insecticide, their cocoon protects them. When people and pets return to the house, adults emerge from their cocoons and immediately begin to seek a blood meal. They jump on cats, dogs, and even people.

Although it may appear that a cat just returned from boarding brought fleas to your home, it is also very possible that a sudden emergence of adult fleas may account for the fleas present.

What are Giardia?

Giardia are sometimes confused with worms because they invade the gastrointestinal tract and can cause diarrhea. They are not worms; instead, they are one-celled parasites classified as protozoa. Most cats that are infected with *Giardia* do not have diarrhea or any other clinical signs. When the eggs (cysts) are found in the stool of a cat without diarrhea, they are generally considered a transient, insignificant finding. However, in kittens and debilitated adult cats, they may cause severe, watery diarrhea that may be fatal.

Giardia: 750 x actual size
(after Kofold and Christiansen)

How did my cat get Giardia?

The cat becomes infected with *Giardia* when it swallows the cyst stage of the parasite. Once inside the cat's intestine, the cyst goes through several stages of maturation and replication. Eventually, the cat is able to pass infective cysts in the stool. These cysts lie in the environment and can infect other cats. They may also be transmitted through drinking *infected* water.

How is giardiasis diagnosed?

Giardiasis is diagnosed by performing a microscopic examination of a stool sample. The cysts are quite small and usually require a special floatation medium for detection, so they are not normally found on routine fecal examinations. Occasionally, the parasites may be seen on a direct smear of the feces. A blood test is also available for detection of antigens (cell proteins) of *Giardia* in the blood. This test is probably more accurate than the stool exam, but it requires several days to get a result from the laboratory performing the test.

How is giardiasis treated?

The typical drug used to kill *Giardia* is metronidazole, an antibiotic-type drug. It is given for 5 - 7 days. Other drugs are also used if diarrhea and dehydration occur. If metronidazole is not effective, others are available.

Can humans become infected with Giardia?

Giardia can also cause diarrhea in humans. Therefore, environmental disinfection is important. The use of chlorine bleach, one cup in a gallon (500 ml in 4 liters) of water, is effective if the surfaces and premises can be safely treated with it. Remember to use gloves for your protection and to let the bleach-water air dry before allowing the cat access so that it does not irritate its paws.

The death of a cherished pet creates a sense of loss for adults and produces a predictable chain of emotions. The stages of grief are typically denial, sadness, depression, guilt, anger, and, finally, relief (or recovery). However, the effects on children vary widely depending upon the child's age and maturity level. The basis for their reaction is their ability to understand death.

Two and Three Year Olds

Children who are two or three years old typically have no understanding of death. They often consider it a form of sleep. They should be told that their pet has died and will not return. Common reactions to this include temporary loss of speech and generalized distress.

The two or three year old should be reassured that the pet's failure to return is unrelated to anything the child may have said or done. Typically, a child in this age range will readily accept another pet in place of the dead one.

Four, Five, and Six Year Olds

Children in this age range have some understanding of death but in a way that relates to a continued existence. The pet may be considered to be living underground while continuing to eat, breathe, and play. Alternatively, it may be considered asleep. A return to life may be expected if the child views death as temporary. These children often feel that any anger they had for the pet may be responsible for its death. This view should be refuted because they may also translate this belief to the death of family members in the past. Some children also see death as contagious and begin to fear that their own death (or that of others) is imminent. They should be reassured that their death is not likely.

Manifestations of grief often take the form of disturbances in bladder and bowel control, eating, and sleeping. This is best managed by parent-child discussions that allow the child to express feelings and concerns. Several brief discussions are generally more productive than one or two prolonged sessions.

Seven, Eight, and Nine Year Olds

The irreversibility of death becomes real to these children. They usually do not personalize death, thinking it cannot happen to themselves. However, some children may develop concerns about death of their parents. They may become very curious about death and its implications. Parents should be ready to respond frankly and honestly to questions that may arise.

Several manifestations of grief may occur in these children, including the development of school problems, learning problems, anti-social behavior, hypochondriacal concerns, or aggression. Additionally, withdrawal, over attentiveness, or clinging behavior may be seen. Based on grief reactions to loss of parents or siblings, it is likely that the symptoms may not occur immediately but several weeks or months later.

Ten and Eleven Year Olds

Children in this age range generally understand death as natural, inevitable, and universal. Consequently, these children often react to death in a manner very similar to adults.

Adolescents

Although this age group also reacts similarly to adults, many adolescents may exhibit various forms of denial. This usually takes the form of a lack of emotional display. Consequently, these young people may be experiencing sincere grief without any outward manifestations.

 HEARTWORM DISEASE

I thought that only dogs got heartworms. Are heartworms common in cats?

We typically consider heartworms to be a parasite affecting dogs. However, in reality, many cats become infected with heartworms.

How are heartworms transmitted?

One of the larval (immature worm) stages of the heartworm is carried by mosquitoes. When a mosquito carrying heartworm larvae bites a cat, the larvae are deposited under the cat's skin. The larvae then begin a long migratory process through the tissues, eventually reaching the heart. They complete their migration and mature to adult heartworms within a period of several months. Their life span as adults in the cat's heart is about 1 - 2 years, during which time they may release larvae (microfilaria) into the blood stream of the cat. Another mosquito may then take blood from the cat, at the same time picking up larvae which can be passed to another cat.

Are these the same heartworms that affect dogs?

Yes, they are. The determination of whether a dog or a cat becomes infected is based solely on the mosquito's choice of its next meal.

What are the signs of heartworm disease in a cat?

For many months, there may be little or no apparent change in the cat. However, as the adult heartworms grow to a length of 6 inches (15 cm) or more, the heart may become strained. We see some of these cats in heart failure; they are very weak and having trouble breathing. Strangely, some cats with heartworms have a history of vomiting with no signs of heart failure. Another presentation of cats with heartworms is sudden death. The pumping action of the blood sends some of the worms or blood clots out of the heart and into the lungs. If the main arteries going to the lungs (the pulmonary arteries) become blocked, the cat will die suddenly. Finally, coughing and sporadic respiratory (breathing) difficulty can be a sign of heartworm disease in cats.

What is the difference in a cat having heartworms and a cat having heartworm disease?

Cats can tolerate a few adult heartworms in the heart for several months. However, as the number of worms increases or the worms increase in size, the cat begins to show the clinical signs that we just discussed. The presence of clinical signs related to heartworms constitutes heartworm disease.

Are there differences in feline heartworm disease and canine heartworm disease?

Since the cat is not a normal host for heartworms, some variations do exist. These are the basis for important differences in diagnosing and treating feline heartworm disease.

Dogs often have 30 or more worms present; however, many cats have only 2 - 4 adult worms in the heart. Adult heartworms live 3 - 4 years in the dog's heart but only 1 - 2 years in the cat's heart. Dogs are able to produce large numbers of microfilaria (babies) into the blood circulation; cats usually do not produce any. Dogs have changes in the shape of the heart and pulmonary arteries as seen on radiographs (x-rays). Their pulmonary arteries become tortuous (curved) and enlarged. However, cats will usually have normal shaped hearts with pulmonary arteries that are blunted, presumably related to partial obstructions due to the presence of adult worms. Dogs usually have a persistent rise in eosinophils, a normal white blood cell which can be associated with parasitic infection. Cats have an eosinophil increase that occurs briefly within a few months of infection. By the time clinical signs are present, most cats have a normal eosinophil count.

How is heartworm infection diagnosed in cats?

Because of some of the differences just mentioned, the typical approach to diagnosing heartworms in dogs is not always successful in cats. The antigen test to detect specific heartworm proteins is often ineffective because at least 4 adult female heartworms must be present for it to yield positive results; cats often do not have that many. Since the cat has few, if any, microfilaria, the test to detect microfilaria in the blood is often negative. An elevated eosinophil count is helpful in dogs but will probably be normal in cats. Even the clinical signs seen in dogs are not very reliable in cats, especially when you consider that vomiting in cats may be related to many other disorders other than heartworms.

When heartworms are suspected, the heartworm antigen test is generally performed first. If it is negative, radiographs of the heart and pulmonary arteries are made. If those are negative, an ultrasound examination of the heart may allow us to actually see the heartworms in some cats. A blood count looking for a rise in eosinophils is often part of the diagnostic evaluation. Sometimes a diagnosis of heartworm disease is made with the best evidence available even though it is not absolutely firm.

How are heartworms treated in cats, and how likely is my cat to survive?

The differences between dogs and cats also impact the approach to treatment. Dogs are treated with a relatively new drug to kill the adult heartworms. However, this drug is toxic to most cats so it is not used for feline heartworm infection. The drug that was used in the past to treat heartworms in dogs is an arsenic-containing drug. It has been used in cats, but there are also many toxic reactions seen. It is safer than the new drug for dogs, but it will still produce a fatal reaction in many cats.

When the adult heartworms die, they are carried to the lungs by the pumping action of the heart. Dogs occasionally have problems with the dead worms lodging in the pulmonary arteries and lungs; coughing for a few days occurs, but it subsides within a few more days. However, cats' pulmonary arteries are so much smaller than that of dogs, that a few worms can cause total arterial obstruction and death within a few minutes. About one-third of cats given the arsenic-containing drug will die due to toxicity or obstruction of the pulmonary arteries. Acute pulmonary edema (sudden onset of fluid in the lungs) is another potentially lethal consequence of treating cats with the arsenical agent.

Another approach is to treat the signs of heart failure, put the cat on a drug to prevent further heartworms from developing, and wait 1 - 2 years for the adult worms to die of old age. This approach is not without failure because a heartworm-infected cat can develop a pulmonary artery obstruction at any time and die acutely. However, the overall success rate (number of cats surviving) is probably greater with symptomatic treatment than when the arsenic-based drug is given to treat the heartworms. However, one situation exists that does make the drug treatment more desirable, when the signs of heart failure cannot be successfully controlled, and the cat is obviously declining.

What about heartworm prevention for cats?

Dogs commonly receive one of several drugs to prevent heartworm infection. Because these drugs are generally considered safe and effective, there are growing numbers of experts who suggest routine administration of heartworm prevention drugs to cats with potential exposure to mosquitoes, especially if they have had heartworms in the past.

HOOKWORM INFECTION

What are hookworms?

Hookworms are parasites which get their name from the hook-like mouthparts they use to attach to the intestinal wall. They are only about 1/8" (3 mm) long and so small in diameter that you have to be looking very carefully to see them. Despite their small size, they suck large amounts of blood from the tiny vessels in the intestinal wall. A large number of hookworms can cause anemia. This problem is most common in kittens, but it will occasionally occur in adult cats. In general, cats tend to harbor very few hookworms compared to the number carried by infected dogs.

Hookworm
(3x actual size)

How did my cat get hookworms?

Adult hookworms pass hundreds of microscopic eggs in the cat's stool. The eggs are invisible to the naked eye. Larvae (immature worms) will hatch from the eggs and remain in the soil for weeks or months. If the cat swallows any of these larvae, hookworm infection will be established. The larvae may also burrow through the cat's skin and migrate to the intestine, where they will mature and complete their life cycle.

In dogs, prenatal infection (infection prior to birth) may be a significant problem. Puppies may become infected by the placental blood flow and then later through the mother's milk. Prenatal infection has not been demonstrated to occur in kittens.

What kinds of problems do hookworms cause for my cat?

For cats, the most significant problems appear related to intestinal distress and anemia. Blood loss results from the parasite sucking blood from intestinal capillaries. A blood transfusion may be needed in some cats because of the rather severe anemia which can be produced by hookworms. The presence of pale gums, diarrhea, or weakness might suggest the need to specifically determine the cat's red blood cell count. Some cats experience significant weight loss with hookworm infection.

In dogs, skin irritation and itching can be one of the common signs of a heavily infested environment. The larvae burrow into the skin and cause the dog a great deal of discomfort. The most common hookworm of cats does not appear to have this type of burrowing behavior.

How is hookworm infection diagnosed?

Hookworms are diagnosed with a microscopic examination of a small stool sample. Since the eggs are produced on a daily basis, hookworm infection is usually fairly easy to diagnose.

How are the hookworms treated?

There are several very effective drugs that will kill hookworms. These are given by injection or orally and have few, if any, side-effects. However, these drugs only kill the adult hookworms. Therefore, it is necessary to treat again in about 2 - 4 weeks to kill any newly formed adult worms that were larvae at the time of the first treatment.

Since the cat's environment can be laden with hookworm eggs and larvae, it may be necessary to treat it with a chemical to kill them. There are several available that are safe to use on grass.

Are feline hookworms infectious to people?

The type of hookworms which infect cats do not infect humans; however, the larvae can burrow into human skin. This causes itching, commonly called ground itch, but the worms do not mature into adults. Direct contact of human skin to moist, infected soil is required. Fortunately, this occurs rarely if normal hygiene practices are observed.

What can be done to control hookworm infection in cats and to prevent human infection?

- All new kittens should be treated by 2 - 3 weeks of age. To effectively break the life cycle of the most common intestinal parasites, kittens should be dewormed on the schedule recommended by the veterinarian.

- Prompt deworming should be given when any parasites are detected; periodic deworming may be appropriate for cats at high risk for reinfection.

- All cat feces should be disposed of promptly, especially in yards, playgrounds, and public parks.

- Strict hygiene is important, especially for children. Do not allow children to play in potentially contaminated environments.

 HYPERTENSION

What is hypertension?

Hypertension is a medical term that means high blood pressure.

I thought hypertension was caused by a stressful lifestyle. My cat certainly does not have that.

Hypertension in people is related to several factors, including a lifestyle that constantly produces stress. Not all of the causes of hypertension in cats have been identified. However, it does not appear that psychological stress plays a role in development of this disease as it does in humans.

How do I know if my cat has hypertension?

The most common clinical presentation of feline hypertension is sudden blindness. This occurs because high pressure in the blood vessels of the retina causes the retina to detach. Affected cats have widely dilated pupils that do not constrict when exposed to bright light. These cats run into objects in their path because most of them have no vision at all.

What causes hypertension in cats?

We have identified two major causes of feline hypertension. The first is kidney failure. The second is heart disease.

How does kidney failure lead to the development of hypertension?

The kidneys are filters that remove waste products from the blood. As a cat gets older, the kidneys undergo normal aging changes, including the slow accumulation of scar tissue. This scar tissue causes the kidneys to shrink in size. With every heartbeat, about 20% of the blood pumped out is delivered to the kidneys. When the kidney shrinks due to the accumulated scar tissue, it is harder for the blood to filter through. There is a backup of blood into the arteries and an increase in blood pressure.

One study found that about 60% of cats in old-age kidney failure had hypertension. Elderly cats not in actual kidney failure may also have hypertension by the same mechanism.

How does heart failure cause hypertension?

Not all forms of heart failure cause hypertension. However, there are at least two forms that have been shown to cause hypertension in cats. Hypertrophic cardiomyopathy is a disease of the heart muscle with an unknown cause. It makes the heart muscle thicken, resulting in blood being pumped more forcefully. This increase in cardiac output of blood results in hypertension. Hyperthyroidism is another cause of heart disease that may cause hypertension.

What is hyperthyroidism, and how does it cause hypertension?

The thyroid is a gland located in the neck. It plays a very important role in regulating the body's rate of metabolism. Hyperthyroidism is a disorder characterized by the overproduction of thyroid hormone.

When excessive amounts of thyroid hormone are in the circulation, the body's metabolism speeds up greatly. Many organs are affected by this disease, including the heart. The heart is stimulated to pump faster and more forcefully, much like hypertrophic cardiomyopathy. This results in a greater output of blood and high blood pressure. About 80% of cats with hyperthyroidism have high blood pressure, although most of them do not have blood pressures high enough to cause blindness.

Hyperthyroidism is a fairly common disease of older cats. Although the thyroid gland enlarges, it is usually a non-malignant change (benign). Less than 2% of hyperthyroid cases involve a malignant change in the gland.

How is hypertension diagnosed?

Hypertension is suspected in any cat with a sudden onset of blindness, kidney failure, heart disease (especially hypertrophic cardiomyopathy), or hyperthyroidism. If any of these are diagnosed, the cat's blood pressure will be checked, if the equipment is available. If a sudden onset of blindness occurs and the blood pressure is found to be abnormally high, the other conditions are considered as possible underlying causes. This means that radiographs (x-rays) of the chest are taken and blood tests are performed for kidney and thyroid function.

Why don't all veterinarians have blood pressure testing equipment?

Blood pressure is determined with a device that can detect blood flow in arteries. However, the cat has very small arteries compared to humans. Therefore, the standard blood pressure equipment used on humans will not work on cats. Only two blood pressure machines have been found reliable in cats. One costs several hundred dollars and the other several thousand. Thus, the expense in purchasing this equipment, coupled with the relative infrequency of hypertension, makes ownership of blood pressure equipment prohibitive for many veterinarians.

Is there a way to treat it?

There are several drugs that are very effective in treating hypertension in humans. However, none of these are approved for feline hypertension. Veterinarians have found that some of these drugs are effective in cats. Although research is still ongoing to determine the most effective drugs, several have been found that will lower the cat's blood pressure.

How successful is treatment?

If the cat has blindness due to detached retinas, a medical emergency exists. If the retinas remain detached for more than a day or two, they probably will not return to their proper position and become functional again. Therefore, the key to successful treatment is rapid diagnosis and early administration of the proper administration to lower blood pressure.

If the cat has kidney, heart, or thyroid disease, it is also important to treat those aggressively. Hyperthyroidism is curable, but hypertrophic cardiomyopathy and old-age kidney failure are not. However, even those can be managed successfully in many cats.

What is likely to happen in the long term?

If blood pressure can be lowered quickly, some blind cats regain their sight. If blood pressure can be maintained in the normal range, these cats will retain their sight. However, the underlying disease that caused hypertension must also be cured or controlled. Long-term success depends on whether or not this is possible.

 HYPERTHYROIDISM

What is hyperthyroidism?

The thyroid is a gland located in the neck. It plays a very important role in regulating the body's rate of metabolism. Hyperthyroidism is a disorder characterized by the overproduction of thyroid hormone. When excessive amounts of thyroid hormone are in the circulation, the body's metabolism speeds up greatly.

Hyperthyroidism is a fairly common disease of older cats. Although the thyroid gland enlarges, it is usually a non-malignant (benign) change. Less than 2% of hyperthyroid cases involve a malignant change in the gland.

What does this do to the cat?

The typical cat with hyperthyroidism is middle aged or older; on the average, affected cats are about 10 years of age. The rapid rate of metabolism causes the cat to lose weight. It tries to compensate for this with an increased appetite. In fact, some of these cats have a ravenous appetite and will literally eat anything in sight! Despite the increased intake of food, most cats gradually lose weight. The weight loss may be so gradual that some owners will not even realize it has occurred. Affected cats usually drink a lot of water and urinate a lot. There may be periodic diarrhea, and the hair coat may be unkempt. As the disease progresses, the cat's appetite may decline to the point of anorexia.

How is hyperthyroidism diagnosed?

The disease is most commonly diagnosed by determining the blood level of one of the thyroid hormones; the hormone most frequently measured is T_4. Usually, the T_4 level is so high that there is no question as to the diagnosis. Occasionally, a cat suspected of having hyperthyroidism will have T_4 levels within the range of normal cats. In this case, a second test, called a T_3 Suppression Test, is performed. If this is not diagnostic, a thyroid scan can be performed at a veterinary referral center.

Is this disease treatable?

Because less than 2% of these cats have cancerous growths of the thyroid gland, treatment is usually very successful. There are three choices for treatment; any one of them could be the best choice in certain situations. Many factors must come into consideration when choosing the therapeutic option for a particular cat.

- **Radioactive iodine**. The most effective way to destroy the abnormal tissue is with radioactive iodine therapy. This requires one to three weeks of hospitalization at a veterinary clinic licensed to administer radiation therapy. This treatment is often limited to veterinary teaching institutions because of governmental regulations regarding radioactive materials. Usually, the expense will be greater than for the other options.

- **Surgery**. Surgical removal of the affected thyroid lobe(s) (thyroidectomy) is also very effective. Because hyperthyroid cats are usually over 10 years of age, there is a degree of risk involved. However, the risk is much less than most people think, as long as the cat is otherwise healthy. Tests are done before surgery to evaluate the cat and predict the chances for complications. If the disease involves both lobes of the thyroid gland, two surgeries may be required, depending on the surgeon's choice of procedures. In many cats, only one thyroid lobe is abnormal, so only one surgery is needed.

- **Oral medication**. Administration of an oral drug, methimazole, can control the effects of the overactive thyroid gland. Some cats have reactions to the drug, but that number is fairly small (less than 20%). However, the side-effects may begin as late as six months after the beginning of treatment and can include vomiting, lethargy, anorexia, fever, and anemia. Methimazole does not destroy the abnormal thyroid tissue, but rather prevents the production of excess thyroid hormone. Therefore, the drug must be given for the remainder of the cat's life. Periodic blood tests must be done to keep the dosage regulated. This type of treatment is appropriate for the cat who is a poor surgical risk due to other health problems.

If I elect to have surgery for my cat, what is the procedure?

If surgery is the treatment method chosen, the cat is put on methimazole for one to four weeks before surgery. This treatment should cause the ravenous appetite to subside, and your cat will probably gain weight. Some cats also have a very fast heart rate and may be medicated before surgery with another drug. After one to two weeks, another T_4 level in the blood is measured.

The operation is performed in a sterile operating room and the cat is under general anesthesia. An incision is made along the neck just below the throat and the enlarged thyroid gland is removed. The skin is sutured together. The cat is generally hospitalized for one night following surgery and returns home feeling quite well. S/he should eat normally after returning home.

Can hyperthyroidism occur again?

Recurrence is a possibility in some cats. Recurrence is uncommon after radioactive iodine therapy. When surgery is performed, the chance of recurrence is slightly greater. It is usually not possible to surgically remove all of the cells from the abnormal thyroid gland. If those remaining cells grow, the disease may recur. However, this occurs less than 10% of the time and usually after 2 - 4 years. Another possibility is that one side of the thyroid gland appeared normal at the time of surgery so it was not removed. Then, months or years later, it may become abnormal.

I think my cat is too old for anything but treatment with the oral medication. Do you agree?

Many owners of cats with hyperthyroidism are hesitant to have radiation therapy or surgery because of their cat's advanced age. But remember, old age is not a disease. The outcomes following both surgery and radiation therapy are usually very positive, and most cats have a very good chance of returning to an excellent state of health.

 ## INFLAMMATORY BOWEL DISEASE

What is inflammatory bowel disease?

Inflammatory Bowel Disease (IBD) is a chronic disease of the intestinal tract. Occasionally, the stomach is involved. Most affected cats have a history of recurrent or chronic vomiting and/or diarrhea. During periods of vomiting or diarrhea, the cat may lose weight but is generally normal in other ways. As a rule, most affected cats eat well (or even have an increased appetite) and appear normal.

What causes this disease?

The cause of IBD is poorly understood. In fact, it appears that there may be several causes. Whatever the cause(s), the end result is that the lining of the intestine is invaded by inflammatory cells. An allergic-type response is then set in place within the bowel lining. This interferes with the ability of the cat to digest and absorb nutrients.

For some cats, dietary components are speculated to play a role in initiation of the disease. Bacterial proteins may be involved in other cases. In most instances, an underlying cause cannot be identified.

How is IBD diagnosed?

There are two ways to diagnose IBD. The first method is a biopsy of the affected part of the stomach or intestine. The preferred technique is to use a flexible endoscope which allows access to the lining of the stomach, small intestine, and colon. If the site of inflammation involves any of these locations, a confirmed diagnosis is achieved. Sometimes, the small intestine may be difficult to enter because of the cat's small size; in these cases, surgical biopsy may be needed. Fortunately, this is rarely necessary. The second method of diagnosis is a therapeutic trial involving administration of particular drugs, along with certain dietary changes. Since not all cats respond to the same drugs, the trial may involve a series of a number of drugs and may take several weeks. Also, different diets may be tried, depending on which part of the bowel appears most involved. These diets include hypoallergenic, low residue, or high fiber foods. The cat is monitored during the therapeutic trial for a decrease in clinical signs and, in some cases, weight gain.

Is IBD treatable?

When a diagnosis of IBD is made, the cat is placed on a hypoallergenic, low residue or high fiber diet for 8 weeks or more. This helps to identify the contribution of dietary components to the problem. Although diet is not a common cause of the disease, it is an inexpensive and effective way to treat IBD if an acceptable food is found. If the dietary trial does not offer any improvement, medication is used to control (not cure) the problem. Since not all cats respond to the same medication, a series of drug trials may be necessary.

What is the prognosis?

Once the appropriate drugs or diet are determined, many cats are maintained on these for life, although dosages of the drugs may eventually be decreased. Occasionally, a cat will be able to stop drug therapy at some point.

Most cats do well for many years; others require alterations in therapy every few months. Unfortunately, a few cats will ultimately become totally resistant to treatment.

 KIDNEY FAILURE

What is meant by the term "Chronic Kidney Failure"?

Presumably, the term "chronic kidney failure" suggests that the kidneys have stopped working and are, therefore, not making urine. However, by definition, kidney failure is the inability of the kidneys to remove waste products from the blood. This definition can occasionally create confusion because some will equate kidney failure with failure to make urine. Kidney failure is NOT the inability to make urine. Ironically, most cats in kidney failure are actually producing large quantities of urine, but the body's wastes are not being effectively eliminated.

When is this likely to happen in my cat?

The typical form of chronic kidney failure is the result of aging; it is simply a "wearing out" process. For most cats, the early signs occur at about 10 - 14 years of age.

What changes are likely to occur in my cat?

The kidneys are nothing more than filters. When aging causes the filtration process to become inefficient and ineffective, blood flow to the kidneys is increased in an attempt to increase filtration. This results in the production of more urine. To keep the cat from becoming dehydrated, due to increased fluid loss in the urine, thirst is increased so the cat drinks more water. Thus, the early clinical signs of kidney failure are increased water consumption and increased urine production. The clinical signs of more advanced kidney failure include loss of appetite, depression, vomiting, diarrhea, and very bad breath. Occasionally, ulcers will be found in the mouth.

How is chronic kidney failure diagnosed?

The diagnosis of kidney failure is made by determining the level of two waste products in the blood: blood urea nitrogen (BUN) and blood creatinine. The urinalysis is also needed to complete the study of kidney function. Although BUN and creatinine levels reflect kidney failure, they do not predict it. A cat with marginal kidney function may have normal blood tests. If that cat is stressed with major illness or surgery, the kidneys may fail, sending the blood test levels quickly into the abnormal range.

Since this is basically just a wearing out process, can it be treated with anything other than a kidney transplant?

Yes it can. We must recognize that your cat's kidneys have reached this point due to aging, so they will never be normal again, but many cats still have enough functional kidney tissue so treatment can be very rewarding. Treatment is in two phases. The first phase is to "restart" the kidneys. Large quantities of intravenous fluids are given to "flush out" the kidneys. This flushing process, called diuresis, helps to stimulate the kidney cells to function again. If enough functional kidney cells remain, they may be able to adequately meet the body's needs for waste removal. Fluid therapy includes replacement of various electrolytes, especially potassium. Other important aspects of initial treatment include proper nutrition and drugs to control vomiting and diarrhea.

What can I expect from this phase of treatment?

There are three possible outcomes from the first phase of treatment:

1) The kidneys will resume functioning and continue to function for a few weeks to a few years.

2) The kidneys will resume functioning during treatment but fail again as soon as treatment stops.

3) Kidney function will not return. Unfortunately, there are no reliable tests that will predict the outcome.

If the first phase of treatment is successful, what happens next?

The second phase of treatment is to keep the kidneys functioning as long as possible. This is accomplished with one or more of the following, depending on the situation:

- **A high quality, low protein diet.** This helps to keep the blood tests as close to normal as possible, which usually makes your cat feel better. A commercially prepared food that has the quantity and quality of protein needed by your cat is recommended.

- **Potassium supplementation.** Potassium is lost in the urine when urine production becomes excessive. A potassium supplement will replace that loss. Low potassium levels have been shown to further reduce kidney function. This is the second reason that a potassium supplement is recommended.

- **A phosphate binder.** One of the secondary things that occurs in kidney failure is an elevation of the blood's level of phosphorus. This also contributes to lethargy and poor appetite. Certain drugs will bind excess phosphates in the intestinal tract so they are not absorbed, resulting in lower blood levels of phosphorus.

- **Fluids given at home.** Once your cat is stabilized, fluids can be given under the skin (subcutaneously). This serves to continually "restart" the kidneys as their function begins to fail again. This is done once daily to once weekly, depending on the degree of kidney failure. Although this might not sound like something you can do, you will be surprised at how easily the technique can be learned and how well most cats will tolerate it.

- **A drug to regulate the parathyroid gland and calcium levels.** Calcium and phosphorus must remain at about a 2:1 ratio in the blood. The increase in blood phosphorus level, as mentioned above, stimulates the parathyroid gland to increase the blood calcium level by removing it from bones. This can be helpful for the sake of the normalizing calcium:phosphorus ratio, but it can make the bones brittle and easily broken. Calcitriol™ can be used to reduce the function of the parathyroid gland and to increase calcium absorption from the intestinal tract.

- **A drug to stimulate the bone marrow to produce new red blood cells.** The kidneys produce erythropoietin, a hormone that stimulates the bone marrow to make red blood cells. Therefore, many cats in kidney failure have a low red blood cell count, anemia. Epogen™ a synthetic form of erythropoietin, will correct the anemia in most cats. Unfortunately for some cats, the drug cannot be used long term because the immune system recognizes the drug as "foreign" and will make antibodies (immune proteins) against it.

How long can I expect my cat to live?

The prognosis is quite variable depending on response to the initial stage of treatment and your ability to perform the follow-up care. However, we encourage treatment in most situations because many cats will respond and have a good quality of life for up to 4 years.

O wning a cat can be an extremely rewarding experience, but it also carries with it quite a bit of responsibility.

How should I introduce my new kitten to its new environment?

A cat is naturally inclined to investigate its new surroundings. At first, you should limit the cat's area of exploration so that these natural tendencies do not create an unmanageable situation. After confining the cat to one room for the first few days, you should slowly allow access to other areas of the home.

What type of playing should I expect from a kitten?

Stimulating play is important during the first week. Stalking and pouncing are important play behaviors in kittens and have an important role in proper muscular development. If given a sufficient outlet for these behaviors with toys, your kitten will be less likely to use family members for these activities. The best toys are lightweight and movable. These include wads of paper and small balls. Kittens should always be supervised when playing with string or ribbons to avoid swallowing them. Any other toy that is small enough to be swallowed should also be avoided.

Can I discipline a kitten?

Disciplining a young kitten may be necessary if its behavior threatens people or property, but harsh punishment should be avoided. Hand clapping and using shaker cans or horns can be intimidating enough to inhibit undesirable behavior. However, remote punishment is preferred. Remote punishment consists of using something that appears unconnected to the punisher to stop the problem behavior. Examples include using spray bottles, throwing objects in the direction of the kitten to startle (but not hit) it, and making loud noises. Remote punishment is preferred because the kitten associates punishment with the undesirable act and not with you.

When should my kitten be vaccinated?

There are many diseases that are fatal to cats. Fortunately, we have the ability to prevent many of these by the use of very effective vaccines. In order to be effective, these vaccines must be given as a series of injections. Ideally, they are given at about 6 - 8, 12, and 16 weeks of age, but this schedule may vary somewhat depending on several factors.

The routine vaccination schedule will protect your kitten from five diseases: distemper panleukopenia (sometimes called 'cat distemper'), three respiratory organisms (rhinotracheitis/FVR, calicivirus, and chlamydia), and rabies. The first four are included in a combination vaccine that is given at 6 - 8, 12, and 16 weeks old. Rabies vaccine is given at 12 or 16 weeks of age. Leukemia vaccine is necessary if your cat does or will go outside or if you have another cat that goes in and out since this deadly disease is transmitted by contact with other cats, especially when fighting occurs. A vaccine is also available for protection against feline infectious peritonitis (FIP); this vaccine is probably not necessary for all cats and is recommended in selected situations.

Why does my kitten need more than one vaccination for feline distemper, upper respiratory infections, and leukemia?

When the kitten nurses its mother, it receives a temporary form of immunity through its mother's milk. This immunity is in the form of proteins called antibodies. For about 24 - 48 hours after birth, the kitten's intestine allows absorption of these antibodies directly into the blood stream. This immunity is of benefit during the first few weeks of the kitten's life, but, at some point, this immunity fails and the kitten must be able to make its own long-lasting immunity. Vaccinations are used for this purpose. As long as the mother's antibodies are present, vaccinations do not "take." The mother's antibodies will neutralize the vaccine so the vaccine does not get a chance to stimulate the kitten's immune system.

Many factors determine when the kitten will be able to respond to the vaccines. These include the level of immunity in the mother cat, how much of the antibody has been absorbed, and the number of vaccines given the kitten. Since we do not know when an individual kitten will lose the short-term immunity, we give a series of vaccinations. We hope that at least two of these will fall in the window of time when the kitten has lost the immunity from its mother but has not yet been exposed to disease. A single vaccination, even if effective, is not likely to stimulate the long-term immunity which is so important.

Rabies vaccine is an exception to this, since one injection given at the proper time is enough to produce long-term immunity.

Do all kittens have worms?

Intestinal parasites are common in kittens. Kittens can become infected with parasites almost as soon as they are born. For example, the most important source of roundworm infection in kittens is the mother's milk.

The microscopic examination of a stool sample will usually help to determine the presence of intestinal parasites. This exam is recommended for all kittens, if a stool sample can be obtained. Even if a stool sample is not possible, the use of a deworming product that is safe and effective against several of the common worms of the cat is recommended. It is important that deworming be repeated in about 3 - 4 weeks, because the deworming medication only kills the adult worms. Within 3 - 4 weeks the larval stages will have become adults and will need to be treated. Cats remain susceptible to reinfection with hookworms and roundworms. Periodic stool analysis and/or deworming throughout the cat's life may be recommended for cats that go outdoors.

Tapeworms are the most common intestinal parasite of cats. Kittens become infected with them when they swallow fleas because the eggs of the tapeworm live inside the flea. When the cat chews or licks its skin as a flea bites, the flea may be swallowed. The flea is digested within the cat's intestine; the tapeworm hatches and then anchors itself to the intestinal lining. Therefore, exposure to fleas may result in a new infection which can occur in as little as two weeks. Cats may also become infected with tapeworms if they hunt and eat mice.

Cats infected with tapeworms will pass small segments of the worms in their stool. The segments are white in color and look like grains of rice. They are about 1/8 inch (3 mm) long and may be seen crawling on the surface of the stool. They may also stick to the hair under the tail. If this occurs, the segments will dry out, shrink to about half their size, and become golden in color.

Tapeworm segments do not pass every day or in every stool sample; therefore, inspection of several consecutive bowel movements may be needed to find them. A stool sample may be examined at a clinic with negative results and then you may find them the next day. If you find them at any time, please notify your veterinarian so the appropriate drug for treatment can be provided.

There are lots of choices of cat foods. What should I feed my kitten?

- Diet is extremely important in the growing months of a cat's life, and there are two important criteria that should be met in selecting food for your kitten.

  We recommend a NAME-BRAND FOOD made by a national cat food company (not a generic or local brand), and a form of food MADE FOR KITTENS. This should be fed until your kitten is about 12 months of age. In the United States, we recommend that you only buy food which has the AAFCO certification. Usually, you can find this information very easily on the label. AAFCO is an organization which oversees the entire pet food industry. It does not endorse any particular food, but it will certify that the food has met the minimum requirements for nutrition. Most of the commercial pet foods will have the AAFCO label. Generic brands often do not have approval. In Canada, look for foods approved by the Canadian Veterinary Medical Association (CVMA).

- Feeding a dry, canned, or semi-moist form of cat food is acceptable. Each has advantages and disadvantages. Dry food is definitely the most inexpensive. It can be left in the cat's bowl at all times. If given the choice, the average cat will eat a mouthful of food about 12 - 20 times per day. The good brands of dry food are just as nutritious as the other forms. As a rule, most veterinarians will recommend dry food for your kitten.

- Semi-moist and canned foods are also acceptable. However, both are considerably more expensive than dry food. They often are more appealing to the cat's taste; however, they are not more nutritious. If you feed a very tasty food, you are running the risk of creating a cat with a finicky appetite. In addition, the semi-moist foods are high in sugar.

- Table foods are not recommended. Because they are generally very tasty, cats will often begin to hold out for these and not eat their well-balanced cat food. If you choose to give your kitten table food, be sure that at least 90% of its diet is good quality commercial kitten food.

- We enjoy a variety of things to eat in our diet. However, most cats actually prefer not to change from one food to another unless they are trained to do so by the way you feed them. Do not feel guilty if your cat is happy to just eat one food day after day, week after week.

- Commercials for cat food can be very misleading. If you watch carefully you will notice that commercials promote cat food on one basis, TASTE. Nutrition is rarely mentioned. Most of the "gourmet" foods are marketed to appeal to owners who want the best for their cats; however, they do not offer the cat any nutritional advantage over a good quality dry food, and they are far more expensive. If your cat eats a gourmet food very long, it will probably not be happy with other foods. If it needs a special diet due to a health problem later in life, it is very unlikely to accept it. Therefore, we do not encourage feeding gourmet cat foods.

How do I insure that my kitten is well socialized?

The socialization period for cats is between 2 and 12 weeks of age. During that time, the kitten is very impressionable to social influences. If it has good experiences with men, women, children, dogs, other cats, etc., it is likely to accept them throughout life. If the experiences are absent or unpleasant, it may become apprehensive or adverse to any of them. Therefore, during the period of socialization, we encourage you to expose your cat to as many types of social events and influences as possible.

What can be done about fleas on my kitten?

Many of the flea control products that are safe on adult cats are not safe for kittens less than 4 months of age. Fleas do not stay on your kitten all of the time. Occasionally, they will jump off and seek another host. Therefore, it is important to kill fleas on your new kitten before they become established in your house. Be sure that any flea product you use is labeled safe for kittens.

If you use a flea spray, your kitten should be sprayed lightly. For very young or small kittens, it is safest to spray a cotton ball and use that to wipe the flea spray on the kitten. Flea and tick dip is not recommended for kittens unless they are at least 4 months of age. Remember, not all insecticides that can be used on dogs are safe for cats and kittens.

Can I trim my kitten's sharp toe nails?

Kittens have very sharp toe nails. They can be trimmed with your regular finger nail clippers or with nail trimmers made for dogs and cats. If you trim too much, you will cut into the quick of the nail which will bleed and be painful. If this happens, neither you nor your cat will want to do this again. Therefore, a few points are helpful:

- If your cat has clear or white nails, you can see the pink of the quick through the nail so it is easy to avoid.

- If your cat has black nails, you will not be able to see the quick so only cut 1/32" (1 mm) of the nail at a time until the cat begins to get sensitive. The sensitivity will usually occur before you are into the blood vessel. With black nails, it is likely that you will get too close on at least one nail.

- If your cat has some clear and some black nails, use the average clear nail as a guide for cutting the black ones.

- When cutting nails, use sharp trimmers. Dull trimmers tend to crush the nail and cause pain even if you are not in the quick.

- You should always have styptic powder available. This is sold in pet stores under several trade names, but it will be labeled for use in trimming nails.

What are ear mites?

Ear mites are tiny insect-like parasites that live in the ear canal of cats (and dogs). The most common sign of ear mite infection is scratching of the ears. Sometimes the ears will appear dirty because of a black material in the ear canal; this material is sometimes shaken out. The instrument that is used for examining the ear canals, an otoscope, has the necessary magnification to see the mites. Sometimes, mites are found by taking a small amount of the black material from the ear canal and examining it with a microscope. Although they may leave the ear canals for short periods of time, they spend the vast majority of their lives within the protection of the ear canal. Transmission generally requires direct ear-to-ear contact. Ear mites are common in litters of kittens if their mother has ear mites.

Why should I have my female cat spayed? *Spaying or ovariohysterectomy is the removal of the uterus and the ovaries. It offers several advantages:*

1) The female's heat periods result in about 2 - 3 weeks of obnoxious behavior. This can be quite annoying if your cat is kept indoors. Male cats are attracted from blocks away and, in fact, seem to come out of the woodwork. They seem to go over, around, and through many doors. Your cat will have a heat period about every 2 - 3 weeks until she is bred.

2) It has been proven that as the female dog gets older, there is a significant incidence of breast cancer and uterine infections if she has not been spayed. Spaying before she has any heat periods will virtually eliminate the chances of either. There is mounting evidence to believe that this is also true of cats.

3) Spaying prevents unplanned litters of kittens.

4) If you do not plan to breed your cat, we strongly recommend that she be spayed before her first heat period. This can be done anytime after she is 5 months old.

Why should I have my male cat neutered?

Neutering or castration offers several advantages. Male cats go through a significant personality change when they mature. They become very possessive of their territory and mark it with their urine to ward off other cats. The tom cat's urine develops a very strong odor that will be almost impossible to remove from your house. They also try to constantly enlarge their territory which means one fight after another. Fighting results in severe infections and abscesses and often engenders rage in your neighbors. We strongly urge you to have your cat neutered at about 6 to 9 months of age. If he should begin to spray his urine before that time, he should be neutered immediately. The longer he sprays or fights, the less likely neutering will stop it.

If I choose to breed my cat, when should that be done?

If you plan to breed your cat, she should have at least one or two heat periods first. This allows her to mature physically and she will be a better mother without so much physical drain. Breeding is not recommended after 5 years of age unless she has been bred prior to that. Having her first litter after 5 years of age is more physically draining to her and increases the chances of her having problems during the pregnancy and/or delivery. Once your cat has had her last litter, she should be spayed to prevent the female problems older cats have.

My kitten is already becoming destructive with her nails. What can be done?

There are four options that you should consider: frequent nail clipping, nail shields, surgical declawing, and tendonectomy.

1) The nails may be clipped according to the instructions above. However, your cat's nails will regrow and become sharp again in about 4 - 7 days. Therefore, to protect your property, it will be necessary to clip them one to two times per week.

2) There are some commercially available products that are called nail caps. These are generally made of smooth plastic and attach to the end of the nail with a special glue. The nails are still present, but the caps prevent them from causing physical harm. After 2 - 4 weeks the nails will grow enough that the caps will be shed. At that time, you should be prepared to replace them.

3) Surgical declawing is the removal of the nail at its base. This is done under general anesthesia and there is very little post-surgical discomfort, especially when it is performed on a kitten. Contrary to the belief of some, this surgery does not cause lameness or psychological damage. Actually, a declawed cat will not realize the claws are gone and will continue to "sharpen" the claws as normal without inflicting damage to your furniture. This surgery can be done as early as 12 weeks of age or anytime thereafter. It can also be done the same time as spaying or neutering. Once declawed, your cat should always live indoors since the ability to defend itself is compromised.

4) Tendonectomy is the surgical removal of a small part of the tendon on the bottom of each toe. This tendon is needed to make the nail extend. The cat retains its nails, but it cannot extend them for sharpening and scratching. The only disadvantage of this procedure is that the nails continue to grow and may grow into the pads. Therefore, the nails should be clipped every 7 to 14 days.

You can also consider ways of modifying behavior which may prevent the cat from scratching furniture in the house or being destructive.

What is megacolon?

The last part of gastrointestinal tract is a tubular organ called the colon. It is the main part of the large bowel. The colon serves as a site for absorption of water and storage of fecal material. It is continuous with the rectum. The walls of the colon contain muscles which are stimulated to contract by nerves from the spinal cord. When the colon contracts, fecal material is pushed out of the body. If the nerves to the colon do not function properly, the muscles of the colonic wall will not contract properly. If this happens, the muscles stretch, and the colon enlarges in diameter. In addition, the fecal material is not moved out of the body and severe constipation may result. This massive enlargement of the colon and the resulting constipation is called megacolon. The colon may have a diameter 3 - 4 times that of a normal cat.

How does it occur?

An injury to the spinal cord can result in formation of megacolon. Also, mechanical obstruction caused by tumor, foreign bodies, hairballs, and strictures can lead to megacolon. However, in most cases, we cannot determine the reason that the nerves to the colon stop functioning. This disease generally occurs in middle-aged to older cats but has also been seen in cats only 3 - 4 years old.

How is it treated?

Usually, a medical approach is tried first, with surgery reserved for unresponsive cases. This involves the use of laxatives, stool softeners, colon wall stimulants, and high fiber diets. These do not correct the underlying cause, but they do allow fecal material to pass so the cat does not become constipated and ill.

The medical approach may be successful for several months or years but will generally fail at some time. When this happens, surgery must be considered. A procedure called subtotal colectomy removes the non-functioning part of the colon. Although this procedure involves removal of most of the colon, the anal sphincter (valve) is left intact, so the cat should not lose bowel control.

Can the cat function without its colon?

Since one of the colon's primary responsibilities is to remove excess fluid from the fecal material, the cat that has had a subtotal colectomy will have rather soft stools immediately after surgery. In addition, there may be several bowel movements each day. However, after 1 - 2 months, most cats have soft, but formed, stool and average 3 bowel movements every 2 days. There should be no loss of fecal control.

What is meant by the term "Chronic Nasal Discharge"?

When a cat has a discharge from its nose that lasts more than 2 months, it is considered chronic. The discharge may be thin and clear like water (serous), thick and yellow or green like pus (purulent), bloody (sanguinous or hemorrhagic), or a combination.

What causes a chronic nasal discharge?

Chronic nasal discharge is not a diagnosis; rather, it is a term that describes the signs of disease in the nose and frontal sinuses. Almost all disease conditions that occur in the nose will cause irritation and inflammation to the lacy bones in the nose, called turbinates. The presence of disease in the nose is called rhinitis. The turbinate bones are easily distorted and destroyed. When that happens, bacteria that normally live in the nose grow rapidly, causing a secondary bacterial infection.

The frontal sinuses are hollow cavities in the skull and are located just above the eyes. They are connected to the nasal cavity by a small canal. Most diseases that occur in the nasal cavity have the ability to move through these canals into the frontal sinuses. When the sinuses become involved and develop inflammation, this is called sinusitis.

Chronic nasal discharge may result from several disorders involving the sinuses and nasal cavity. These include:

- Chronic viral infection
- Chronic bacterial infection
- Chronic fungal infection
- Food allergy
- Nasal foreign body (e.g. grass seed)
- Nasal tumor
- Inflammatory polyp

What tests should be done to make an accurate diagnosis?

There are several diagnostic tests that should be done for a cat with a chronic nasal discharge. A blood profile will often detect underlying diseases that can contribute to a nasal disease. Testing for the feline leukemia virus (FeLV) and the feline immunodeficiency virus (FIV) is important because these viruses have the ability to suppress the cat's immune system, making recovery from normally mild infections difficult (or even impossible).

It is very important to make radiographs (x-rays) of the skull. Special positions are necessary to view the nasal cavity and frontal sinuses. These require sedation or a short-acting anesthetic. A nasal flush is a diagnostic procedure used to collect material from deep within the nasal cavity. This material can be studied under the microscope (cytology) and can also be cultured. Although it is not particularly traumatic to the cat, anesthesia is required, so this procedure is usually done in conjunction with radiographs. This allows more than one procedure to be done while the cat is under anesthesia.

Some veterinarians have a specialized instrument called an endoscope which allows the veterinarian to actually look inside the nose, as well as to examine the back of the throat and the area around the soft palate. In order to pass this small flexible tube into the area of interest, anesthesia is required.

There are some diseases that can only be diagnosed with a biopsy of material deep within the nasal cavity. A biopsy requires recovery of an actual piece of tissue, so surgery is often required for this procedure.

Foreign objects within the nasal passage can sometimes be detected with radiographs. If a foreign body is suspected but not visualized, endoscopy may be helpful, depending on where the foreign body is located. For some cases, exploratory surgery of the nasal cavity is needed.

Allergic conditions (such as food allergy) are not detected by any of the above tests. This cause of chronic nasal discharge is diagnosed with a food trial. A food trial consists of feeding a special, hypoallergenic diet for 4 - 8 weeks and evaluating the cat's response.

As you can see, it may require several days or weeks of testing to determine the cause of a chronic nasal discharge. When the diagnosis remains elusive, more sophisticated tests may be required. Veterinarians unable to perform these tests often refer the cat to a specialist.

How is a chronic viral infection treated?

Respiratory viruses which can infect the nose may persist and lead to long term viral rhinitis/sinusitis. No drugs are available to kill them so this type of infection is often incurable but some cats will respond to a booster dose of a viral respiratory vaccine.

How is a chronic bacterial infection treated?

Administration of antibiotics alone is usually unsuccessful in curing bacterial infections of the nose and sinuses because the bacteria have become entrapped within the turbinates, and re-infections are frequent. Although many cats improve while taking antibiotics, cortisone, or antihistamines, they will relapse when these drugs are discontinued. The use of drugs that stimulate the immune system and the surgical removal of the turbinates have been successful in some cats. However, others do not respond well. Overall, the prognosis is guarded.

How is a chronic fungal infection treated?

The most common fungal infection in the nose is caused by *Cryptococcus neoformans*. Because some of the drugs used to treat this organism are quite expensive and will occasionally cause adverse effects, they are not used unless a firm diagnosis is made. Fortunately, the newer antifungal drugs have fewer significant side-effects and many cats with fungal diseases can be successfully treated. If the cat is infected with the feline leukemia virus or feline immunodeficiency virus, the outcome will usually be less favorable.

How is a food allergy treated?

It is necessary to perform a food trial to make a diagnosis of food allergy. If the chronic nasal discharge responds to a hypoallergenic diet, that diet is usually continued to the exclusion of other foods. In some cases, other foods are tried to see if there may be several foods acceptable. If an acceptable diet is found, the prognosis is good.

How is a nasal foreign body treated?

When a piece of grass or other foreign material lodges in the nasal cavity, the membrane which lines the nose produces large amounts of mucus in response to the irritation. In addition, affected cats will sneeze violently in an attempt to expel the foreign body.

If the foreign body cannot be sneezed out, the veterinarian must take steps to remove it. When a nasal foreign body is suspected but cannot be seen on radiographs or with an endoscope, exploratory surgery may be needed. If it is found and removed, the prognosis is good.

How is a tumor treated?

Most nasal tumors are malignant. Complete surgical removal is very unlikely, so chemotherapy or radiation therapy must be considered. Unfortunately, many nasal tumors do not respond to either treatment, so the prognosis is poor. However, when surgery is performed to obtain tissue for biopsy, most surgeons remove as much of the tumor as possible. Following this procedure, the cat may be greatly relieved of the nasal discharge and remain improved for several months. However, in almost all cases, the tumor can be expected to recur.

How is an inflammatory polyp treated?

Inflammatory polyps are non-cancerous masses of tissue that are composed of inflammatory cells. Extensive surgery is often successful in removing much of the polyp, but re-growth is assured if not all of it can be removed. Since these often begin in the internal ear and grow down the Eustachian tube into the back of the nose, their removal can require extensive surgery that may not be completely successful. The prognosis for an inflammatory polyp is guarded because the entire polyp cannot be removed in most cases.

Raising an orphaned kitten is a noble and rewarding experience. The bonding that will occur in the first few days will likely last for many years. However, orphaned kittens are very fragile; raising them requires jumping numerous hurdles. Do not be disappointed if you are not successful.

What problems am I likely to encounter?

Several critical problems must be addressed in caring for orphaned kittens. Among these are chilling, dehydration, and hypoglycemia (low blood sugar). These problems are interrelated and may often exist at the same time. Close observation and prompt attention if any of these problems develop are essential to survival. Of course, proper feeding of the orphaned kitten is extremely important.

Chilling

Chilling in newborn kittens can lead to significant mortality. A kitten will dissipate far more body heat per pound of body weight than an adult cat. The normal newborn kitten depends upon radiant heat from its mother to help maintain its body temperature. In the absence of the mother, various methods of providing heat, such as incubators, heat lamps, or hot water bottles can be used.

Rectal temperatures in a normal newborn kitten range from 95 to 99°F (35 to 37.2°C) for the first week, 97 to 100°F (36.1 to 37.7°C) for the second and third weeks, and reach the normal temperature of an adult 100 to 102°F (37.7 to 38.9°C) by the fourth week.

When the rectal temperature drops below 94° F (34.4°C), the accompanying metabolic alterations are life-threatening. Therefore, immediate action is necessary to provide the warmth the kitten needs to survive. A healthy newborn can usually survive chilling if warmed slowly.

During the first four days of its life, the orphaned kitten should be maintained in an environmental temperature of 85 to 90°F (29.4 to 32.2°C). The temperature may gradually be decreased to 80 °F (26.7°C) by the seventh to tenth day and to 72°F (22.2°C) by the end of the fourth week. If the litter is large, the temperature need not be as high. As kittens huddle together, their body heat provides additional warmth.

 Caution: Too rapid warming of a chilled kitten may result in its death.

Dehydration

The lack of regular liquid intake or the exposure of the kitten to a low humidity environment can easily result in dehydration. The inefficiency of the digestion and metabolism of a chilled kitten may also lead to dehydration and other changes such as those discussed in this book.

Experienced breeders can detect dehydration by the sense of touch. Two signs of dehydration are the loss of elasticity in the skin and dry and sticky mucous membranes (gums) in the mouth.

An environmental relative humidity of 55 to 65 percent is adequate to prevent drying of the skin in a normal newborn kitten. However, a relative humidity of 85 to 90 percent is more effective in maintaining kittens if they are small and weak.

Caution: *The environmental temperature should not exceed 90°F (32.2°C) when high humidity is provided. A temperature of 95°F (35°C) coupled with relative humidity of 95 percent can lead to respiratory distress.*

Hypoglycemia (low blood sugar levels)

Signs of hypoglycemia (abnormal decrease of sugar in the blood) are severe depression, muscle twitching and sometimes convulsions. If a kitten shows signs of hypoglycemia, a solution containing glucose will have to be administered. A few drops of corn syrup on the tongue can be life-saving.

What do I feed my orphaned kitten?

Total nutrition for the newborn orphans must be supplied by a milk replacer until the kittens are about three weeks of age. At this age, the kittens are ready to start nibbling moistened solid food.

Preferred diets:

A commercial kitten milk replacer or for short-term emergencies you can make up a diet:

- 1 cup of milk
- 1 tablespoon corn oil
- 1 pinch of salt
- egg yolks (no whites)
- Blend mixture uniformly

Is the temperature of the food important?

Since the newborn may have trouble generating enough heat to maintain its body temperature, the milk replacer should be warmed to 95 to 100°F (35 to 37.8°C) for the best results. Testing the milk replacer's temperature on one's forearm (as for babies) is generally accurate enough. The milk replacer should be about the same temperature as one's skin or slightly warmer. As the kittens grow older, the milk replacer can be fed at room temperature.

How do I feed my kitten?

- **Spoon feeding** is slow and requires great patience. Each spoonful must be slowly "poured" into the kitten's mouth to prevent liquids from entering the lungs. The kitten's head must not be elevated, or the lungs may fill with fluids. Newborn kittens usually do not have a well-developed gag reflex to signal this.

- **Dropper feeding** accomplishes the same result as spoon feeding but is somewhat cleaner and generally speedier.

- **Baby bottles** made for kittens can be used quite successfully in most situations. The size of the hole in the nipple is critical for success. If the bottle is turned upside down and milk replacer drips from the nipple, the hole is too large. Use of this nipple may cause drowning of the kitten. If the bottle is turned upside down and milk replacer comes out only after considerable squeezing of the bottle, the hole is too small. Use of this nipple will result in the kitten becoming discouraged and refusing to nurse. The hole is the proper size if the bottle is turned upside down and milk replacer drips from the nipple with minimal squeezing of the bottle.

- **Tube feeding** is the easiest, cleanest and most efficient method of hand feeding. However, it requires proper equipment and technique to prevent putting milk replacer into the kitten's lungs. If bottle feeding is not successful, your veterinarian will supply the equipment and demonstrate the proper technique. This is not a difficult procedure, so do not hesitate to ask about it if it is needed.

When and how much do I feed?

Commercial milk replacers have directions on their labels for proper amounts to feed. It is necessary for the kitten's weight to be obtained properly in ounces or grams. The amounts on the labels are based on the kitten getting only the milk replacer. The amounts given are also for a 24 hour period. That quantity should be divided by the number of feedings per 24 hours. Four meals, equally spaced during a 24 hour period, are ample for feeding a kitten when adequate nutrients are provided. Six or more feedings may be necessary if the kitten is small or weak. Hand feeding can generally be ended by the third week and certainly by the fourth. By this time the kitten can consume food, free-choice, from a dish (*see below*).

How do I get the kitten to urinate and defecate?

The kitten's genital area must be stimulated after feeding to cause urination and defecation. The genital area should be massaged with a moist cloth or cotton ball to stimulate action. This cleaning should continue during the first two weeks. If this procedure is not followed, the kitten may become constipated.

When does the kitten start to eat from a bowl?

By three weeks, the kitten can start to eat food from the dish along with the milk replacer. A gruel can be made by thoroughly mixing a kitten food (canned or dry) with the milk replacer to reach the consistency of a thick milk shake. The mixture should not be too thick at first or the kitten will not consume very much. As the consumption of food increases, the amount of milk replacer can be gradually decreased. By four to four and one-half weeks, the orphaned kitten can consume enough moistened solid food to meet its needs. It is better to avoid starting a kitten on a baby food regimen. This creates extra work and can also create a finicky eater. Many such foods will not meet the nutritional needs of a growing kitten.

Should my kitten be treated for worms?

We routinely treat kittens for worms at 3 and 6 weeks of age. We need to see the kitten at the appropriate ages so that it can be accurately weighed.

When is the first vaccination given?

The first vaccination is normally given to kittens at 6 - 8 weeks of age. However, if your kitten did not nurse from its mother during the first 2 - 3 days after birth, there will be no protective immunity passed to it. If that is the case, the first vaccination should be given at about 2 - 3 weeks of age.

PANCREATITIS

What is pancreatitis?

The pancreas is a vital organ which lies on the right side of the abdomen. It has two functions: 1) to produce enzymes which help in digestion of food and, 2) to produce hormones, such as insulin. When the pancreas becomes inflamed, the disorder is called pancreatitis. It is a disease process that is seen commonly in the dog and occasionally in the cat. There is no age, sex, or breed predisposition.

There are two main forms of acute (sudden onset) pancreatitis: 1) the mild, edematous form and, 2) the more severe, hemorrhagic form. A few cats that recover from an acute episode of pancreatitis may continue to have recurrent bouts of the acute disease, known as chronic, relapsing pancreatitis. The associated inflammation allows digestive enzymes to spill into the abdominal cavity; this may result in secondary damage to surrounding organs, such as the liver, bile ducts, gall bladder, and intestines.

What causes it?

The cause of pancreatitis is not known. There may be more than one cause. In dogs, it is often associated with a rich, fatty meal or the administration of cortisone; however, these associations have not been found with feline pancreatitis.

Under normal conditions, the digestive enzymes produced by the pancreas are activated when they reach the small intestines. In pancreatitis, the enzymes are activated prematurely in the pancreas instead of in the small intestines. This results in digestion of the pancreas itself and, thus, the clinical signs begin. The clinical signs of pancreatitis are often variable, and the intensity of the disease will depend on the quantity of enzymes that is prematurely activated.

What are the clinical signs?

The diagnosis of pancreatitis is based on three criteria: clinical signs, laboratory tests, and radiographic (x-rays) and/or ultrasound examination. The disease is typically manifested by nausea, vomiting, fever, abdominal pain, and diarrhea. If the attack is severe, acute shock, depression, and death may occur. Laboratory tests usually reveal an elevated white blood cell count; however, an elevated white blood cell count may also be caused by many other things besides pancreatitis. The elevation of pancreatic enzymes in the blood is probably the most helpful criteria in detecting pancreatic disease, but many cats with pancreatitis will have normal levels. Radiographs and ultrasound studies may show an area of inflammation in the location of the pancreas. Unfortunately, many cats with pancreatitis will elude detection with any of these tests. Consequently, the diagnosis of pancreatitis may be tentative in many cases.

How is pancreatitis treated?

The successful management of pancreatitis will depend on early diagnosis and prompt medical therapy. The mild form of the disease is best treated by resting the pancreas from its role in digestion. The only way to "turn off" the pancreas is to withhold all oral fluids and food. This approach is accompanied by intravenous fluids to maintain normal fluid and electrolyte balance. In addition, anti-inflammatory drugs are sometimes administered. The presence of shock necessitates the immediate and intense use of intravenous fluids and systemic antibiotics.

Will my cat recover?

The prognosis depends on the extent of the disease when presented and a favorable response to initial therapy. Cats that present with shock and depression have a very guarded prognosis. Most of the mild forms of pancreatitis have a good prognosis.

Will there be any long-term problems?

There are two possible long-term results that may follow severe or repeated pancreatitis. If a significant number of cells that produce digestive enzymes are destroyed, a lack of proper food digestion may follow. This is known as pancreatic insufficiency and can be treated with daily administration of enzyme tablets or powder in the food. If a significant number of cells that produce insulin are destroyed, diabetes mellitus can result. This can usually be treated with daily injections of insulin. However, most cats recover with no long-term effects.

What is panleukopenia?

Literally the name panleukopenia means a decrease in numbers of all the white blood cells. White blood cells are so important in defending the animal against infections and disease. In severe panleukopenia white blood cell numbers may drop from the normal of several thousand per millilitre of blood to just a few hundred. This makes the cat very vulnerable to other infections.

What is the cause?

Panleukopenia is caused by a virus of the Parvovirus family (a similar, but distinct virus causes Parvovirus disease in dogs). This virus is one of the toughest viruses known and is only killed by strong disinfectants such as 2 percent household bleach. The virus can survive in some environments for weeks and months.

How is infection transmitted?

The virus is shed in all excretions, particularly feces, of infected cats. It can be ingested directly or transferred to a susceptible cat via contaminated water, feed bowls, or even on shoes. The incubation period from infection until clinical signs develop is typically 3 to 5 days, seldom longer than a week.

What are the clinical signs?

There is some variation but typically cats experience a very deep depression or listlessness which may progress to collapse. Vomiting and diarrhea are frequent and the diarrhea may contain blood. The hair coat quickly becomes dull and rough, and the skin loses its elasticity (dehydration). Often cats with panleukopenia have other infections because their immune system is damaged. They can often have purulent discharges from eyes and nose. The disease picture then has some similarities to distemper in dogs, hence, the name 'feline distemper'. But it is really a very different disease.

Can panleukopenia be treated?

As for most viruses, there is no specific treatment. Antibiotics are ineffective against viruses, but they are helpful in controlling the bacterial infections which can be a problem in these cats because of their lack of white cells and reduced immunity. Dehydration and shock are the life-threatening components of panleukopenia and intravenous fluid therapy and intense nursing is critical. If the animal can be supported through the acute illness, prognosis for a full recovery is good.

How can I protect my cat against panleukopenia?

Fortunately excellent vaccines are available and are routinely recommended by veterinarians as part of a vaccination program. It is important that kittens receive more than one dose because of the uncertain interference of maternal antibody (see Vaccination Failures p. 111). The immunity conferred by panleukopenia vaccine is generally strong and long-lasting but it decreases with time, and faster in some cats than others. Therefore annual 'booster' vaccinations are highly recommended.

The aging cat goes through a number of changes which result in the ultimate failure of various body organs and systems. Recent research has identified a problem related to potassium balance which is common in many older cats. Fortunately, the problem is treatable. As a result, many elderly cats are now living longer and healthier lives.

What is potassium, and why is it especially important in older cats?

Potassium is found in the cat's blood and within all the cells of the body. It is essential for many functions of cells. Potassium is probably most important for the cells which make up skeletal and cardiac muscle. Severe muscle weakness can result when the body becomes depleted of potassium.

Recently, two important discoveries have been made concerning potassium and older cats. A mild form of hypokalemia (low blood potassium) has been identified in the older cat; it is associated with lethargy and inactivity, a poor appetite and haircoat, and the development of a mild anemia. Formerly, we have considered these to be part of the aging process. Now we know that this process can be reversed with supplementation of potassium. Unfortunately, we do not have a test to conclusively identify these cats because the blood test for potassium is a poor reflection of the body's total store of potassium. Blood potassium may be normal in cats who are actually depleted of potassium within their body's cells. For these cats, a 30 to 45 day trial of potassium is necessary. If response occurs and potassium supplementation is continued, the cat will continue to feel, act, and eat better and will live longer.

The second discovery about low blood potassium is related to the effect of potassium on the kidneys. The kidneys are the organs that usually wear out first in the older cat. As the kidneys become less efficient in removing waste products from the blood, the cat drinks more and more water in an attempt to flush toxins from the body (via the kidneys). An undesired consequence of increased urination is the loss of potassium from the body in the urine. As urine production increases, more and more potassium is lost, eventually leading to hypokalemia. The potassium loss associated with increased urine production has a negative effect on the kidneys. Research has demonstrated that low potassium will depress kidney function. This results in a vicious cycle: declining kidney function results in increased loss of potassium, and the loss of potassium then speeds up the deterioration of the kidneys.

How can my cat benefit by this information?

These important discoveries now allow us to interrupt this vicious cycle by supplementing the cat with potassium. By so doing, kidney function is supported and prolonged, and the cat acts, feels, and eats better at the same time.

How do I give potassium to my cat?

Potassium is available in three forms: 1) a tablet, 2) a powder that can be mixed with canned food, and 3) a tasty gel. All are readily available through veterinarians. Potassium is also sold for human use as a grape-flavored liquid. However, most cats are not fond of the taste of this product. If your cat eats canned food, you should try the powder first. It can be mixed in canned food and will be eaten by most cats. If your cat does not eat canned food and is cooperative about taking pills, you should try the tablets. If these are not successful, the tasty gel is a good approach. Many, but certainly not all, cats will take this readily.

 PYOTHORAX

What is pyothorax?

Pyothorax is an infection that occurs in the pleural space. This space is located between the lungs and the chest wall. The infection produces pus which collects in the pleural space and limits the amount of room available for the lungs to expand. As fluid accumulates, the cat tries to compensate by breathing more rapidly. Because of limited space available for lung expansion, the cat must take very shallow breaths. Pain associated with inflammation in the pleural space (pleuritis) may also contribute to shallow breathing. In addition to respiratory difficulties, the infection in the chest releases toxins into the blood stream creating further stress on the cat. Pyothorax is a very serious illness. If left untreated, the cat will die. Some cats will die even with appropriate treatment.

What causes pyothorax?

The answer to this question is subject to debate. We know that severe dental disease may release bacteria into the blood stream; this blood-borne infection may eventually reach the pleural space. Foreign bodies, such as grass awns, are known to cause pyothorax if they migrate into the chest. Bite wounds through the chest wall are also recognized as a potential cause. However, in most cases, it is impossible to determine what started the infection.

How is pyothorax treated?

The ideal method of treatment involves surgical placement of a drain tube into the pleural space. The tube usually remains in place for several days. Placement of a chest tube offers several advantages, both diagnostic and therapeutic. First, it allows the chest cavity to be more completely emptied than is possible with intermittent drainage by a syringe and needle. Second, it allows cleansing solutions to be flushed into the chest. Third, once a chest tube is in place, the rate of ongoing fluid formation and changes in the character of the fluid can be assessed. Finally, the chest tube is very helpful in preventing further pus accumulation in the chest cavity.

Antibiotic therapy is also a cornerstone of treatment. A sample of the pus is sent to the laboratory for identification of the bacteria and determination of an appropriate antibiotic. Because lab tests can tell us which antibiotic is best, the cat's chances of recovery are greatly improved when the fluid is cultured. Most cats are started on an injectable antibiotic; after improvement occurs and the drain tube is removed, it is usually possible to continue treatment at home with an oral antibiotic.

What are some of the complications of pyothorax?

Cats with other (concurrent) diseases will have a poorer prognosis than cats with no other problems. Of particular significance would be cats infected with the feline leukemia virus or feline immunodeficiency virus. Complications include spread of the infection to other organs and the development of adhesions (or scar tissue) between the lungs and chest wall. Adhesions may lead to reduced lung function in some patients.

How long does treatment take?

Most cats require drainage through the chest tube for about 5 - 10 days. They are almost always hospitalized during that phase of treatment. When pus accumulation stops, the tube is removed, and the cat is sent home to complete treatment. The complete treatment usually takes 4 - 8 weeks. If it is stopped too soon, relapse may occur. However, this does not tend to be a recurring disease, so the long term prognosis is usually very good.

 RABIES

What is rabies?

Rabies is a viral disease which is characterized by severe neurological disturbance. It can affect any warm-blooded species of animal, including of course, people, and is almost always fatal.

What are the signs?

Three stages of the disease are recognized. An early 'prodromal' phase where there may be a marked change in temperament. The quiet cat becomes agitated; the active cat becomes nervous or shy. Other signs include dilated pupils, excessive drooling and snapping at imaginary objects. After 2 or 3 days the 'excitative' phase takes over. There is exaggerated response to any stimulus. Cats may experience bizarre changes in appetite including eating and swallowing sticks, stones or other objects. The animal may roam aimlessly, inflict self-trauma and have a change in vocalization. There will often be vicious, aggressive behavior, even towards the owner. Seizures may occur. Sometimes there is a 'dumb' form of rabies where the animal is extremely depressed, the mouth may gape open with the tongue protruding. A progressive paralysis can occur.

Are there diseases which can be mistaken for rabies?

There are a number of conditions which can cause some of the signs of rabies. A few conditions can be very similar. Confirmation can only be made by laboratory tests, usually post mortem.

How can I catch rabies?

Rabies is very seldom transmitted except by the bite of a rabid animal. Even then the virus is present in the saliva of the infected animal for a limited time. However, if you are bitten by any animal of which you do not know the rabies vaccination status, you should immediately wash the wound thoroughly with soap and water. Try to establish who the owns the animal, and whether the pet is fully vaccinated for rabies. In any case seek medical opinion. Post-exposure rabies treatment with serum and/or vaccine may be recommended. This is very successful when commenced promptly.

What wild animals are most likely to carry rabies?

All mammals can catch rabies but some seem to be much more susceptible than others. Foxes, skunks and raccoons are particularly prone to rabies and one should be very careful if any wild animal seems overly approachable since this is not their usual behavior.

Should I get my cat vaccinated?

Rabies vaccines are very safe and very effective. Therefore it is recommended for all cats. The public health concern is so significant that even totally indoor cats should be vaccinated. Vaccination for rabies is usually done at three to four months of age, and then every one to three years (depending on vaccine and relative risk which your veterinarian will advise).

 RINGWORM

What is ringworm, and what causes it?

Ringworm is a skin disease caused by a fungus (plural: fungi). Because the lesions are often circular, it was once thought to be caused by a worm curling up in the tissue. However, there is no truth to that; it has nothing to do with a worm. There are four fungal species affecting cats which can cause the disease that we call ringworm. These may also affect humans. The fungi live in hair follicles and cause the hair shafts to break off at the skin line. This usually results in round patches of hair loss. As the fungus multiplies, the lesions may become irregularly shaped and spread over the cat's body.

How long does it take to get it?

The incubation period is 10 - 12 days. This means that the exposure to the fungus and thus, the actual infection occurs 10 - 12 days before any lesions occur.

How is it diagnosed?

Diagnosis is made in one of 3 ways: 1) identification of the typical "ringworm" lesions on the skin, 2) fluorescence of infected hairs under a special light (however, only 2 of the 4 species of fungi fluoresce), or 3) culture of the hair for the fungus. The last method is the most accurate, but it may take up to 2 - 3 weeks for the culture to become positive.

How is it transmitted?

Transmission occurs by direct contact between infected and non-infected individuals. It may be passed from dogs to cats and vice versa. It may also be passed from dogs or cats to people and visa versa. If your child has ringworm, he or she may have gotten it from your pet or from another child at school. Adult humans usually are resistant to infection unless there is a break in the skin (a scratch, etc.), but children are quite susceptible. If you or your family members have suspicious skin lesions, check with your family physician.

Transmission may also occur from the infected environment. The fungal spores may live in bedding or carpet for several months. They may be killed with a dilution of chlorine bleach and water (1 pint of chlorine bleach in a gallon of water) (500 ml in 4 liters) where it is feasible to use it.

How is it treated?

There are several means of treatment. The specific method(s) chosen for your cat will depend on the severity of the infection, how many pets are involved, if there are children in the household, and how difficult it will be to disinfect your pets' environment.

- **Griseofulvin.** This is a tablet that is concentrated deep in the hair follicles where it can reach the site of active fungal growth. Griseofulvin should be given daily. Cats with active lesions should receive the tablets for a minimum of 30 days. At that time, your cat should be rechecked to be sure the infection is adequately treated. These tablets are not absorbed from the stomach unless there is fat in the stomach at the time they are given. This can be accomplished by feeding a high fat diet, such as a rich canned cat food or a small amount of fat trimmings from meats (often available at the meat departments of local grocery stores upon request of the butcher) or by allowing the cat to drink some rich cream. This is the most important part of the treatment. If you are not successful in giving the tablets, please call your veterinarian for help.

- **Topical antifungal medication.** Apply one of these products to the affected areas once daily for 10 days. Do not risk getting it in your cat's eyes by treating lesions very near the eye.

- **Baths using an antifungal shampoo.** A bath should be given 3 times on an every other day schedule. Bathe exposed but unaffected pets once. These baths are important in getting the spores off the hairs so they do not drop into the environment and result in re-exposure. A lather should be formed and left on for 5 minutes before rinsing.

- **Lime Sulfur Dip**. This should be done twice weekly for the first two weeks then once weekly for 4 - 6 weeks. Lime sulfur dip should also be applied to other pets (dogs or cats) in the household to prevent them from being affected. If they develop ringworm lesions, they should begin on griseofulvin. You should wear gloves when applying the dip. This is an effective form of treatment, but the dip has an objectionable odor.

- **Ringworm vaccine**. This vaccine helps the cat to develop immunity to the fungus. Other products are still used with it, but its use will hasten recovery. This is especially important if several other pets or children are exposed.

- **Shaving of the cat's hair**. This will remove the infected hair. This is recommended only when the infection is extensive.

What should I expect from treatment?

Treatment will not produce immediate results. The areas of hair loss will get larger before they begin to get smaller. Within 1 - 2 weeks the hair loss should stop, there should be no new areas of hair loss, and the crusty appearance of the skin should subside and the skin look more normal. If any of these do not occur within two weeks, we should see your cat again.

How long will my cat be contagious?

Infected pets remain contagious for about 3 weeks if aggressive treatment is used. Contagion will last longer if only minimal measures are taken of if you are not faithful with the prescribed approach. Minimizing exposure to other dogs or cats and to your family members is recommended during this period.

I have heard that some cats are never cured. Is this true?

When treatment is completed, ringworm should be cured. Although a carrier state can exist, this usually occurs because treatment is not long enough or aggressive enough or because there is some underlying disease compromising the immune system.

 ## ROUNDWORM INFECTION

What are roundworms?

As their name implies, these are worms which have round bodies. On average, they are about 3 - 5 inches (7 - 12 cm) long. They live in the cat's intestines and consume partially digested food. Unlike hookworms, they do not attach to the intestinal wall; rather, they literally swim in their food. Roundworms, sometimes called ascarids, pass moderate numbers of microscopic eggs which are found in the cat's stool. Like hookworm eggs, they must be found with a microscope.

Roundworm
(actual size)

How did my cat get roundworms?

The major source of roundworm infection for kittens is the mother's milk. Roundworm larvae (immature worms) may be present in the queen's mammary glands and milk throughout the period of nursing the kittens.

Both kittens and adult cats may become infected by swallowing roundworm eggs which contain infective larvae. The larvae hatch out in the cat's stomach and small intestine and migrate through the muscle, liver, and lungs. After several weeks, the larvae make their way back to the intestine to mature. When these worms begin to reproduce, new eggs will pass in the cat's stool, and the life cycle of the parasite is completed. Obviously, roundworm eggs passed in one cat's stool may be infectious to other cats. Interestingly, a large number of other animal species have been found to harbor roundworms and represent potential sources of infection for cats. These include cockroaches, earthworms, chickens, and rodents.

What kinds of problems do roundworms cause for my cat?

They are not highly pathogenic (harmful) to adult cats, but large numbers can cause weight loss and a pot-bellied appearance to kittens and weak adults. Decreased appetite, vomiting or diarrhea will be observed on occasion. Kittens will sometimes die with serious roundworm infections.

How is roundworm infection diagnosed?

Roundworms are diagnosed by a microscopic examination of the cat's stool. They pass a moderate number of eggs, so examination of more than one stool sample may be necessary to find them. Occasionally, the mature worms can be found in the cat's stool or vomit.

How are roundworms treated?

Treatment is quite simple. Several very safe and effective drugs are available to kill roundworms in the intestine. Some of these drugs temporarily anesthetize the worms so that they pass out of the cat with a normal bowel movement. The live or dead worms are found in the stool. Because of their large size, they are easily seen. At least two or three treatments are needed; they are typically performed at 2 - 4 week intervals. None of these treatments will kill the immature forms of the worm or the migrating larvae.

The eggs are highly resistant to most commonly used disinfectants and to even harsh environmental conditions. Therefore, removal of the cat's stool is the most effective means of preventing reinfection. A 1% solution of household bleach can be used to remove the sticky outer coating of the eggs, making it easier to rinse them away. This does not, however, kill the eggs. Remember the obvious limitations about where bleach may be safely applied. If bleach is used in the cat's litterbox, be sure to rinse it completely since bleach is potentially toxic to cats.

Are feline roundworms infectious to people?

Yes. The roundworms of both cats and dogs pose a health risk for humans. As many as 10,000 cases of roundworm infection in humans have been reported in one year. Children, in particular, are at risk for health problems should they become infected. A variety of organs may be affected as the larvae migrate through the body. In suitable environments, the eggs may remain infective to humans (and to cats) for *years*.

What can be done to control roundworm infection in cats and to prevent human infection?

- Pregnant queens should be dewormed in late pregnancy to reduce potential contamination of the environment for newborn kittens.

- All new kittens should be treated by 2 - 3 weeks of age. To effectively break the roundworm life cycle, kittens should be dewormed on the schedule recommended by your veterinarian.

- Prompt deworming should be given when any parasites are detected; periodic deworming may be appropriate for cats at high risk for reinfection. Adult cats remain susceptible to reinfection with roundworms throughout their lives.

- Cats with predatory habits should have a fecal examination several times a year. Rodent control is desirable since rodents may serve as a source of roundworm infection for cats.

- Prompt disposal of all cat feces is important, especially in yards, playgrounds, and public parks.

- Stool should be removed from litter-boxes daily, if possible. Litter-boxes can be cleaned with a 1% bleach solution to remove roundworm eggs; rinse well to remove all bleach.

- Strict hygiene is especially important for children. Do not allow children to play in potentially contaminated environments.

TAPEWORM INFECTION

What are tapeworms?

The most common tapeworm of cats (and dogs) is called *Dipylidium caninum*. This parasite attaches to the small intestinal wall by hook-like mouthparts. Adult tapeworms may reach 8 inches (20 cm) in length. The adult worm is actually made up of many small segments about 1/8 inch (3 mm) long. As the tail end of the worm matures, the terminal segments break off and pass into the stool. Occasionally, the mobile segments can be seen crawling near the anus or on the surface of a fresh bowel movement. These segments look like grains of rice and contain tapeworm eggs; the eggs are released into the environment when the segment dries. The dried segments are small (about 1/16", or 2 mm), hard and golden in color. These dried segments can sometimes be seen stuck to the hair around the cat's anus.

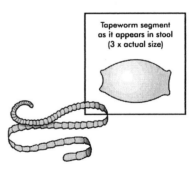

Tapeworm segment as it appears in stool (3 x actual size)

Tapeworm (half actual size)

How did my cat get tapeworms?

First, tapeworm eggs must be swallowed by flea larvae (an immature stage of the flea). Contact between flea larvae and tapeworm eggs is thought to occur most frequently in contaminated bedding or carpet. The life cycle of the tapeworm cannot be completed unless the flea swallows tapeworm larvae. Next, the cat chews or licks its skin as a flea bites; the flea is then swallowed. As the flea is digested within the cat's intestine, the tapeworm hatches and anchors itself to the intestinal lining.

What kind of problems do tapeworms cause for the cat?

Tapeworms are not highly pathogenic (harmful) to your cat. They may cause debilitation and weight loss when they occur in large numbers. Sometimes, the cat will scoot or drag its anus across the ground or carpet because the segments are irritating to the skin in this area. This behavior is much more common in dogs than cats. The adult worm is generally not seen, but the white segments which break away from the tapeworm and pass outside the body rarely fail to get an owner's attention! Occasionally, a tapeworm will release its attachment in the intestines and move into the stomach. This irritates the stomach, causing the cat to vomit the worm. When this happens, a worm several inches in length will be seen.

How is tapeworm infection diagnosed?

Tapeworm infection is usually diagnosed when the white, mobile segments are seen crawling on your cat or in the stool. Tapeworms are not usually detected by the routine fecal examination performed by the veterinarian. Because of this, veterinarians depend on the owner to notify them of possible tapeworm infection in the cat.

How are the tapeworms treated?

Treatment is simple and, fortunately, very effective. A drug which kills tapeworms is given, either orally or by injection. It causes the tapeworm to dissolve within the intestines. Since the worm is usually digested before it passes, it is not visible in your cat's stool. These drugs should not cause vomiting, diarrhea, or any other adverse side-effects.

Control of fleas is very important in the management and prevention of tapeworm infection. Flea control involves treatment of your cat, the indoor environment and the outdoor environment where the cat resides. If the cat lives in a flea-infested environment, reinfection with tapeworms may occur in as little as two weeks. Because the medication which treats tapeworm infection is so effective, return of the tapeworms is almost always due to reinfection from the environment.

How do I tell tapeworms from pinworms?

Tapeworms and pinworms look very similar. However, contrary to popular belief, pinworms do not infect cats or dogs. Any worm segments seen associated with cats are due to tapeworms. Children who get pinworms do not get them from cats or dogs.

Are feline tapeworms infectious to people?

Yes, although infection is not common or likely. A flea must be ingested for humans to become infected with the most common tapeworm of cats. Most reported cases have involved children. The most effective way to prevent human infection is through aggressive, thorough flea control. The risk for infection with this tapeworm in humans is quite small but does exist.

One less common group of tapeworms, called *Echinococcus*, is of particular concern as a threat to human health. These tapeworms cause very serious disease when humans become infected. This parasite is harder to diagnose than the tapeworm caused by fleas because the segments are small and not readily seen. Hunters and trappers in the north central United States and south central Canada may be at risk for infection by this worm if strict hygiene is not observed. Foxes and coyotes (and the wild rodents upon which they prey) are important in the life cycle of this parasite. Dogs and cats may also become infected if they eat rodents carrying the parasite. When eggs of *Echinococcus* are passed in the feces of the dog and cat, humans are at risk for infection. Free-roaming cats and dogs may need to be periodically treated with tapeworm medication. Rodent control and good hygiene are important in preventing the spread of this disease to humans. As with the more common tapeworm, infection with *Echinococcus* is infrequent but possible.

What can be done to control tapeworm infection in cats and to prevent human infection?

- Effective flea control is important.

- Prompt deworming should be given when parasites are detected; periodic deworming may be appropriate for pets at high risk for reinfection.

- All pet feces should be disposed of promptly, especially in yards, playgrounds, and public parks.

- Strict hygiene is important, especially for children. Do not allow children to play in potentially contaminated environments.

 TOXOPLASMOSIS

What is toxoplasmosis?

Toxoplasmosis is a disease caused by a one-celled parasite called *Toxoplasma gondii*, hereafter called the "toxo organism." In humans, it may affect many different organs of the body, causing many different types of clinical signs. The respiratory system is commonly involved and pneumonia may result. The most common finding is a mild, flu-like illness that lasts a few days. Most people recover uneventfully. Even if the patient sees a physician, the illness may still be attributed to the flu unless special blood tests are run.

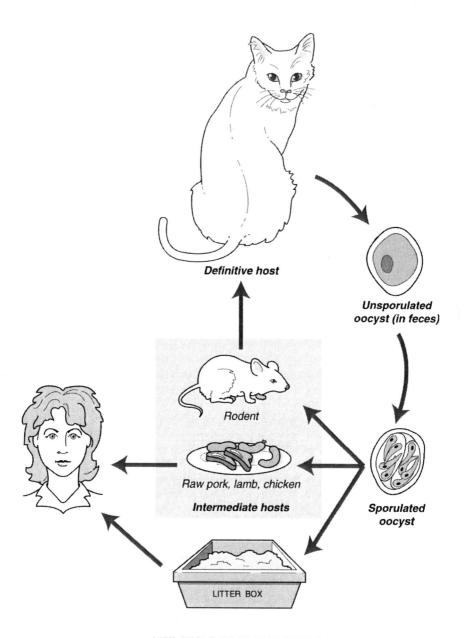

Definitive host

Unsporulated oocyst (in feces)

Rodent

Raw pork, lamb, chicken

Intermediate hosts

Sporulated oocyst

LITTER BOX

LIFE CYCLE OF TOXOPLASMOSIS

How does it relate to pregnant women?

If a pregnant woman contracts toxoplasmosis, it is possible for the toxo organism to affect the unborn baby. It is this form of the disease that has the most dire consequences because the baby may be affected for life.

How common is toxoplasmosis in adults? And how common in cats?

Exposure to the toxo organism will result in the production of antibodies. Antibodies are the defense agents of the immune system and are produced in response to immune system stimulation. The presence of antibodies means that the person or cat has been exposed; it does not necessarily mean that any disease occurred. It is estimated that about 50% of domestic cats in the United States have been exposed to toxoplasmosis. It is also estimated that about 33% of the U.S. population has been exposed. However, those statistics do not mean that 50% of the cats or 33% of humans have had the disease toxoplasmosis. The presence of antibodies only means that exposure to the toxo organism has occurred in the past.

How common is it in babies?

The disease toxoplasmosis occurs in about 140 babies per million births in the United States, or about 14 per 100,000. A like number of children will be infected with the toxo organism at the time of birth and develop disease later in life. Therefore, the combined incidence of congenital and acquired toxoplasmosis in the United States is 28 per 100,000 or 0.028%. Although this is indeed a real disease with dire consequences, it should be noted that its incidence is very small, especially in light of how many people have *Toxoplasma* antibodies.

How is it transmitted?

Although several species may develop the disease toxoplasmosis, including humans and dogs, the organism can only complete its life cycle in the domestic cat. This means that the cat may be infected with the toxo organism and transmit it to other cats or to other species, including humans. However, in order for this to occur the following must happen:

- The cat must be infected with the toxo organism, and most cats are not. In order for this to occur, the cat must eat something infected with it. It is most commonly available to the cat by ingestion of infected mice or infected raw or undercooked meats, especially pork or mutton.

- The cat must be shedding the toxo organism in its feces. This occurs for only about a 10 day period. It usually only occurs once in the cat's lifetime. (In a few situations, the cat may shed the organism again; however, if that occurs, the number of organisms that are shed are so small that transmission is very unlikely.)

- The toxo organism must "incubate" in the cat's feces for 1 - 5 days before it is infective to humans. This "incubation" must occur after the feces leaves the cat's body and have access to oxygen (i.e. in the litter box or in soil).

- The toxo organism must be swallowed by the person being infected. It is not spread to humans through the air.

The toxo organism may also be transmitted to humans by eating raw or undercooked meats, especially pork or mutton. Since many hamburgers from fast-food restaurants are made of beef diluted with pork, most authorities feel that human infection occurs much more frequently by this method than by association with cats. The incidence of toxo antibodies in U.S. veterinarians is not different than that of the rest of the population.

What is involved in testing for toxoplasmosis?

We are frequently asked to test a cat that belongs to a pregnant woman for toxoplasmosis. Pregnant women should know the following concerning toxoplasmosis testing.

A screening test for toxo antibodies can be performed on both the pregnant woman and the cat. A negative result means that the woman (and/or the cat) has not been exposed to the toxo organism. However, it does not infer that either the woman or the cat has any immunity to toxoplasmosis in the event of a future exposure. In fact, it means just the opposite. Both are susceptible to infection.

A single antibody titer that is positive, performed on the woman and/or the cat, means that there has been exposure to the toxo organism in the past or that there is an active infection of toxoplasmosis in progress. In order to know which situation exists, a second test must be run 2 - 4 weeks later.

If the two tests give similar results, there has been an infection in the past and a certain degree of immunity exists.

If the second test is significantly higher that the first, there is a strong possibility that an active case of toxoplasmosis is in progress.

It is very important that both tests be performed by the same testing laboratory in order to properly compare results.

The direct means of documenting the possibility of transmission of toxoplasmosis requires that we microscopically examine a fecal sample from the cat looking for the oocysts (eggs) of the toxo organism. Because these oocysts are very tiny (even under a microscope) and because the cat may not be shedding oocysts today but may do so in the future, multiple examinations must be done during the course of pregnancy, preferably once weekly. This is not a very high yield procedure, meaning that it can be difficult to detect the parasites, and they can be missed by this diagnostic technique.

How can toxoplasmosis be prevented?

There are several practical means of preventing the transmission of toxoplasmosis.

- Do not allow your cat to eat mice or poorly-cooked meat. Feeding a commercial cat food and not allowing your cat outdoors virtually eliminates any possibility of the cat becoming infected.

- Clean all feces from your cat's litter box daily. *Even if the cat's feces is infected with toxo oocysts, they must incubate for 1 - 5 days before becoming infectious.* To be extra safe, do not let a pregnant woman clean the litter box.

- When working in soil (flower beds) that cats might use for defecation, wear gloves to keep from getting oocysts on your hands.

- Avoid eating raw or poorly-cooked meats. Be especially careful of fast-food hamburgers. Since this is probably more of a threat to your baby than your cat, special attention should be paid here.

- Keep children's sandboxes covered. Outdoor cats will frequently use the sandbox for defecation. Even if the feces are scooped out, the sandbox may remain contaminated with parasites.

SUMMARY

- Toxoplasmosis that affects babies is quite rare. (Incidence in the United States is 0.028% of all births). It is frequently referred to as "A Ladies Home Journal Disease." (This magazine was the first widely-read publication to link toxoplasmosis and cats).

- Feeding commercial cat food and keeping your cat indoors so it can not catch mice will prevent spread of toxoplasmosis by your cat.

- Having someone other than a pregnant woman clean out the litter box daily will prevent spread of toxoplasmosis by your cat.

- Transmission from your cat to you requires that you swallow the toxo oocysts that have incubated in your cat's feces for 1 - 5 days. Reasonable personal hygiene should be adequate to prevent that from occurring.

- Toxoplasmosis is transmitted more commonly in the United States via poorly cooked meat than by cats.

- Testing your cat's blood for toxoplasma antibodies is only meaningful if a positive test is followed 2 - 4 weeks later with another test.

- Weekly testing of your cat's feces will more directly detect a cat that is capable of transmitting toxoplasmosis.

What are upper respiratory infections?

There are several conditions that cause cats to sneeze. However, sneezing that lasts more than two days is probably due to a viral upper respiratory infection (URI), similar to a "cold" that we may have. The "upper" part of the name means that the infection is limited to the nose, throat, trachea, and eyes. Lower respiratory infections occur in the lungs but are quite uncommon in cats.

What causes them?

There are 6 known viruses that cause feline URI's. Two of these cause severe infections resulting in loss of appetite, high fever, and ulcers of the tongue and cornea (surface of the eye). These viruses are the feline rhinotracheitis virus (FVR), also called feline herpesvirus, and the feline calicivirus. The other viruses cause mild sneezing for a few days but are rarely a serious problem.

Do upper respiratory infections cause severe illness?

As a rule, the uncomplicated forms of these infections are no more severe than the common cold. However, even mild infections can become life-threatening if secondary bacterial infections occur in the nose, oral cavity, or eyes. Cats so affected may also lose their appetites; this represents the single most serious complication. Once this occurs, the cat will become malnourished and dehydrated. If not corrected soon, many cats will die.

What is involved in treatment?

The first decision in treatment is where it is best to treat your cat - should your cat be hospitalized or treated at home? If the cat is eating, it is preferable to treat it at home. However, if there are other cats at home that are not infected, it may be best to treat it in the hospital to protect the healthy cats. These viruses are very contagious and are spread by sneezing. If your cat is not eating, hospitalization is preferred so that proper antibiotics and nutrition may be administered. If this is done quickly, all but a very few cats will recover completely. If your cat is being treated at home and stops eating, it should be hospitalized for more intense treatment.

Can these infections be prevented?

If a cat has not become infected with the rhinotracheitis virus or calicivirus, vaccination is usually successful in preventing infection. For cats who are already carriers of these viruses, it is still important to vaccinate. Because immunity from vaccination only lasts about 12 - 18 months, annual vaccinations are necessary. If a carrier cat should reactivate the virus and begin shedding, periodic vaccination provides the immune system with a "reminder." This allows the immune system to produce antibodies, the defense agents of the immune system, which can be readily available to begin fighting the infection. Thus, the cat may still develop an URI, but the consequences will be less severe and the recovery will be faster. Even indoor-only cats should be vaccinated since the viruses are air-borne.

Are future infections likely?

Many cats that have infections due to the rhinotracheitis virus or the calicivirus will become carriers. These cats are typically well, but they will have recurrence of sneezing. Cats with the rhinotracheitis virus constantly shed virus, and those with the calicivirus only shed when stressed.

 VACCINATION FAILURES

One of our greatest frustrations is when a cat develops a disease against which it has been vaccinated. There are four basic reasons for this that we shall try to explain.

1) Ineffective vaccine

Strict regulations govern the production and sale of animal vaccines in the United States and Canada. The vaccines made by licensed manufacturers are potent at the time they leave the factory; however, several things may happen to inactivate them. The most common cause of vaccine inactivation is that the vaccines have been allowed to become too warm. Temperature is critical to maintaining potency. If the vaccine gets too warm during shipment to the distributor or while being stored at the distributor, it is inactivated. This is a common problem associated with vaccines purchased by mail or from feed stores. The buyer has no way to determine whether the vaccines were handled properly during shipment to non-veterinary suppliers. Veterinarians routinely refuse to accept shipments of vaccine if the vaccine is warm at the time of arrival.

2) Inherent characteristics of the vaccine

Although most of our vaccines have a very high success rate in cats, none produce immunity in 100% of the vaccinates. The feline leukemia vaccine produces immunity in only 80 - 90% of cats that receive it. The vaccine for some of the feline respiratory viruses produces a high level of immunity, but that immunity lasts only 8 - 10 months in many cats.

3) The cat is not healthy

It is mandatory for the patient's immune system to function properly in order to respond to the vaccine challenge. If the immune system is very immature, it cannot do so. If the patient has a disease that suppresses the immune system, it will not respond. If the patient has a fever, the immune system will be so "occupied" with the fever that it will respond only poorly to vaccine.

4) Interference due to maternal antibodies

When a kitten is born, it receives immunity-producing proteins from its mother. These are called maternal antibodies. Maternal antibodies protect the newborn from the diseases against which the mother was protected. Maternal antibodies only last a few weeks in the kitten; their duration is directly proportional to the level of immunity the mother has. If her immunity level against rabies, for example, is very high, the maternal antibodies for rabies may last up to 4 months. If her level is low, they may persist only 5 or 6 weeks. As long as they are present, the kitten is protected; however, those antibodies also block a vaccine challenge. If a kitten receives a vaccination for rabies before the rabies antibodies are gone, the vaccination is blocked, and no immunity develops. The same holds true for the other components of the vaccines - the temporary immunity received from the mother can interfere with all of the vaccinations.

Ideally, a vaccination should be given just after the maternal antibodies are gone but before the kitten is exposed to the disease-causing virus or bacterium. However, it is not practical to determine just when the maternal antibodies are gone for each of the possible diseases. It can be done, but the expense would be tremendous. A vaccination schedule consists of a series of vaccinations given at regular intervals. The timing of this plan is successful in the vast majority of situations. However, if the maternal antibodies are gone and the kitten is exposed to the disease causing virus or bacterium before the next vaccination occurs, the patient will usually develop the disease.

The solution to this dilemma would be to give more vaccinations in the series. If the premise is known to be infected with a particular disease causing agent, we may recommend vaccinating every 10 to 14 days from age 6 weeks to 16 weeks. The disadvantage for such a plan is the expense. Instead of giving 3 vaccinations in the series, we would be giving 6 or 8, thus the cost would be more than double. The potential benefits and risks of extra vaccinations can be discussed with the veterinarian.

VACCINES AND VACCINATION

What is a vaccine?

The word vaccine comes from the latin word for cow (vacca) and the term was first used in honor of the English country doctor, Edward Jenner. Dr. Jenner discovered that by inoculating the skin of people with a preparation ('vaccine') of material from the common cattle disease, cowpox (or vaccinia), those 'vaccinated' individuals were subsequently protected against the dreaded disease smallpox. Smallpox is caused by a virus closely related to cowpox.

The concept of using a mild infection to protect against a severe disease caused by a related organism, was extended by the famous French scientist, Louis Pasteur. Pasteur and his colleagues were able to produce less harmful ('attenuated') forms of organisms such as rabies which could be used as "vaccines" to induce protection or 'immunity'.

What is 'immunity'?

Immunity is a complex series of defenses by which an animal is able to resist an infection or, at the minimum, resist the harmful consequences of the infection. The main components of these defences are the white blood cells; especially lymphocytes and their chemical products: antibodies and cytokines such as interferon.

All infectious disease organisms (viruses, bacteria, protozoa, fungi, etc.) have specific components called 'antigens'. These antigens cause lymphocytes to respond in a specific way such that each antigen stimulates the production of a mirror-image 'antibody', as well as non-antibody responses called 'cellular immunity'.

Immunity has memory but the memory can fade, sometimes quite rapidly.

Immunity is not absolute. In most cases an animal will still become infected but it can limit the infection, and in the process immunity is 'boosted'. Immunity can sometimes be overcome in cases where there is overwhelming exposure to a high dose of infection, or when the animal is unduly stressed.

What is a live-modified vaccine?

In a live-modified or live-attenuated vaccine the causative organism (virus, bacterium, etc.) has been altered (modified) so that it is no longer harmful ('virulent'), but upon injection or other administration, it will stimulate protective immunity.

What is a killed vaccine?

The organism has been killed ('inactivated') to render it harmless. Killed vaccines often need a helper or 'adjuvant' to stimulate a lasting immune response.

Which is better: live or killed vaccine?

Both have advantages and disadvantages. Your veterinarian takes many circumstances into account in making the choice.

Why a 'needle'?

Some vaccines are given 'locally', for example into the nose, but most require injection so that the maximum take-up of vaccine by the white cells and the immune system is achieved.

Some vaccines are injected into subcutaneous (under-the-skin) sites, others into the muscles (intramuscular). Injections look easy but there are a number of precautions a veterinarian is taking.

Which vaccines are needed in cats?

If your cat led a totally sheltered experience with no exposure to other cats, or no chance that you might bring infection home on your hands or clothes, then vaccination would not be needed. Your vet will assess the relative risks based on your circumstances, and advise you accordingly.

The range of vaccines available includes feline panleukopenia (also called 'enteritis' and 'feline distemper'), the respiratory disease group (rhinotracheitis or FVR, calicivirus and chlamydia, which is sometimes called pneumonitis), feline leukemia, feline infectious peritonitis, and rabies. These vaccines are often available in combinations. These are convenient and avoid extra 'needles'!

Why is more than one dose of vaccine given to kittens?

There are two reasons. First, without complicated testing it is impossible to know when a kitten has lost the immunity it gets from its mother (maternal antibody). An early decline in a kitten's maternal antibody can leave it susceptible to infection at a very young age and a strong maternal immunity can actually interfere with early vaccination (see Vaccination Failure). Second, particularly with killed vaccines, the first dose is a 'priming' dose, and the second dose boosts the response to a higher, longer-lasting immunity.

Why annual revaccinations?

In most properly-vaccinated cats, the immunity should last more than a year, and often several years. However immunity does decline with time, and this decline rate varies with individuals. Therefore to maintain the best immunity in a reasonable way, annual revaccinations have proven very successful.

How long does it take for a vaccine to work?

Within a few hours of vaccination the earliest phases of the immune response are being stimulated. However it is usually 10 to 14 days before a reasonable level of protection is established, and with killed vaccines it may not be until after the second dose is given. Also in young kittens maternal antibody may hinder protection until later in the vaccine series. Therefore it is advisable to keep a recently vaccinated kitten away from other cats until it has finished its vaccination course.

What happens if my cat is unwell when vaccinated?

The veterinary check-up prior to vaccination, and sometimes blood tests pre-vaccination, helps prevent this situation. In most cases it would not have disastrous consequences but it is important that an animal is completely healthy when vaccinated, to ensure proper development of immunity.

Will vaccination make my cat sick?

It is not unusual to detect some lethargy in the day or so after vaccination. In the case of killed vaccines with adjuvants, some thickening or lump formation may occur at the vaccination site. If this is obviously painful or persists for more than a week or so with no decrease in size, consult your veterinarian.

A few cats will develop more severe reactions which are forms of hypersensitivity (allergy). These will usually occur within minutes but may be delayed for a few hours. The cat may have difficulty breathing, salivate, vomit, and scratch or rub its head vigorously. In these situations consult your veterinarian immediately.

What causes vomiting?

Vomiting is not a disease; rather, it is a symptom of many different diseases. Many cases of vomiting are self-limiting after a few days. Less commonly, vomiting may result from a serious illness, such as cancer. Even when vomiting is caused by mild illnesses, it may lead to death of the animal if treatment is not begun early enough to prevent severe fluid and nutrient losses.

How serious is vomiting in cats?

We attempt to determine how sick the cat has become as a consequence of the vomiting. When the cat is systemically ill (i.e., more than one body system is involved), some of the following may be noted:

- Diarrhea
- Dehydration
- Loss of appetite
- Abdominal pain
- High fever
- Lethargy
- Bloody vomiting

What types of tests are performed to find the cause?

If vomiting is associated with several of the above signs, we perform a series of tests in the hope that a diagnosis may be made. When this can be done, more specific treatment may be initiated. Diagnostic tests may include radiography (x-rays) with or without barium, blood tests, biopsies of the stomach and intestinal tract, and exploratory abdominal surgery. Once the diagnosis is known, treatment may include special medications, diets, and/or surgery.

If your cat does not appear systemically ill from the vomiting, the cause may be less serious. Some of the minor causes of vomiting include stomach or intestinal viruses, stomach or intestinal parasites, and dietary indiscretions (such as eating garbage or other offensive or irritating materials). A minimum number of tests are performed to rule out certain parasites and infections. These cases may be treated with drugs to control the motility of the intestinal tract, drugs that relieve inflammation in the intestinal tract, and, often, a special diet for a few days. This approach allows the body's healing mechanisms to correct the problem. Expect improvement within 2 - 4 days; if this does not occur, your veterinarian will make a change in medication or perform further tests to better understand the problem. Please keep your veterinarian informed of lack of expected improvement so that the situation may be managed properly.

Index

023A